prayer energy

prayer energy

Rediscover the power of prayer
to bring about change

Richard Lawrence
with Mark Bennett

CICO BOOKS
LONDON NEW YORK

Published in 2009 by CICO Books
An imprint of
Ryland Peters & Small
20–21 Jockey's Fields
London, WC1R 4BW

519 Broadway, 5th Floor
New York, NY 10012

www.cicobooks.com

10 9 8 7 6 5 4 3 2 1

A CIP catalog record for this book is available from the Library of Congress and the British Library.

ISBN-13: 978 1 906525 52 1

Printed in China

Editor: Marion Paull
Designer: David Fordham
Jacket photography: Patrick Molnar, Getty Images

AUTHOR'S ACKNOWLEDGMENTS
This book could not have been written without
the enormous contribution of Mark Bennett. He
virtually acted as co-author at every stage of this
project and for that I am extremely grateful.

I would like to thank the International Directors
and the Ecclesiastical Synod of The Aetherius
Society for wholeheartedly supporting this project
from the outset, and endorsing the inclusion in
this book of the principles of prayer taught by the
Society's late Founder/President, the Western Master
of yoga, Dr George King (1919–97). I would also
like to thank the International Directors of The
Aetherius Society for granting permission for the
inclusion of extracts from works by Dr King. For
more information about The Aetherius Society,
please visit www.aetherius.org.

I am grateful to Dr John Holder, Steve Gibson,
and Brian Keneipp for their constructive input on
the original manuscript; to Nikki Perrott who
assisted in its preparation; and to Ayub Malik who
assisted Mark Bennett with research.

My thanks go to all those who gave permission
for prayers and quotations to be included, and to
Alyson Lawrence, Chrissie Blaze, and Ray Nielsen
for composing prayers specifically for the book.

Finally, a big thank-you to Liz Dean, Managing
Editor of CICO Books, who was inspired to
initiate this project, together with Cindy Richards,
the Publisher.

www.richardlawrence.co.uk

Contents

PREFACE

the first time I experienced prayer energy was while I was at university and it was to change my life forever.

I was educated at King's School, Canterbury, which is attached to the cathedral. My father was a committed Christian in the Church of England, so religion already played a significant role in my life – but the nature of that role changed dramatically.

When I was fourteen, I woke up one morning wanting to know the meaning of life. It was that sudden. Overnight, I had become aware of an emptiness in the pleasant life I was leading and, although my teenage years were happy—full of friends, parties, music, and all the usual things—the urge to find answers to the big questions never left me.

What was most disappointing was not so much that nobody could provide satisfactory answers, but that they did not seem to care—at least not as I did. This was typified by the response to the flurry of difficult questions I put to one very senior member of the Church of England, who was working at the cathedral while I was at school. His concluding advice was as simple as it was inadequate—"Well, just don't worry about it all. You'll get used to it."

At university, I discovered the path of raja yoga—a system of spiritual development leading to meditation that was catching on at that time. These profound, ancient teachings gave me a sense of peace on an intuitive level, which I had not experienced before, and I felt that this may be what I had been looking for. Soon, however, I found the path that was to change my life.

I went to a lecture given by a PhD student, John Holder, on the Aetherius Society, an organization founded by Dr George King in 1955 to promote world spiritualization. The lecture covered many areas, one of them dynamic prayer. Returning to my hall of residence, I tried out the technique we had been taught, practising for perhaps five or ten minutes. It was amazing – my body was tingling all over as I felt the prayer energy flowing through my aura, although I didn't understand what it was then. I went to bed, expecting the sensation to fade, but it didn't. I lay there for hours, trying in vain to get to sleep. Not having any understanding of what this sensation that was keeping me awake really was, I had no idea of how to stop it.

By 4 a.m., I'd had enough. So I got up, walked the several miles to where the student who had organized the lecture lived, and—with more desperation than good manners—woke him up. But to no avail. He had no idea what was going on. All he could do was tell me how to get in touch with John Holder, which I did the following day. John introduced me to the greatest teachings I have ever encountered, for which I will always be grateful. We became firm friends and remain so to this day.

Finally, I found the answers I had been seeking and dynamic prayer has been a major part of my life ever since. Dr King devised this simple yet powerful technique, based on ancient principles, for anyone to use. A master of yoga, he later became my personal teacher and close friend.

INTRODUCTION

'More things are wrought by prayer
Than this world dreams of.'

ALFRED, LORD TENNYSON

what is prayer?

Prayer is a way of channelling and transmitting energy. It can bring joy, inspiration, healing, peace, exhilaration – and even bliss.

Let's debunk some common misapprehensions right away.

* *It is not a dull duty or a meaningless chore, but a vibrant, living power.*
* *It is not the deluded hope of someone crying out in desperation, but the practical solution to myriad problems.*
* *It is not an act of fear or false piety, but one of courage and true love.*

If prayer were understood and practiced every day by more people, I wholeheartedly believe that not only would those people's lives change, but the whole world would change. Why? Because prayer works. And once the nature of prayer becomes clear and we begin to understand how it works, the confusion and doubt that all too often haunt the would-be prayerful believer are gone.

Everything in creation is manifested through energy. In Indian philosophy this energy is known as *prana*. In China, it is referred to as *qi* (or *ch'i*), in Japan as *ki*. It is akin to the Greek concept of *pneuma* and the Melanesian *mana*. The name is not important, though. What is important is what it is, and what it does. It can be aptly described as "universal life force" because that is exactly what it is—the force of life, which exists throughout the universe. It is life itself. And even more remarkable than this, we can all invoke and use this energy simply by the power of thought. When we want something, the desire makes us magnets for energy. We use our minds, consciously or unconsciously, to direct it to bring about a certain result. This is the power of creative visualization, or intention, but it is not real prayer.

WHAT IS REAL PRAYER?

Real prayer is not a device for trying to get whatever we want. It is an expression of love. To pray properly, we must unchain the shackles of selfishness from our hearts and condition the energy we invoke with the power of love. Think of love as the vehicle in which the energy travels to its destination. As the great yogi Swami Vivekananda put it: "The

Detail of Tangka-Trinle Gyelstshen, 42nd Chief Abbot of Bhutan. Appliqué work with embroidery, 1905.

moment you have succeeded in manufacturing love out of *prana*, you are free."

The efficacy of a prayer is not dependent on the whim or favoritism of a mythical overlord, whom some mistake for the great Divine Source. On the contrary, it is exact in the way that a science is exact. In fact, I would say that it *is* a science—albeit one of which few scientists seem to have much understanding. It is a scientific formula for sending energy, conditioned by love, from the person praying to the focal point of the prayer. How well a prayer works basically depends on:

❖ *How much energy we invoke and send out.*
❖ *How well this energy is conditioned by love.*
❖ *The karma of the situation or condition you are praying for.*

viewed in this light, there is no need to be haunted by the specter of doubt when our prayers don't seem to be answered. Prayer is a natural power—not a superstition. Comments such as "I prayed for world peace for five minutes last night and yet war is still going on, therefore God does not exist" are absurdly superficial. To bring about world peace would require a colossal amount of spiritual energy. In fact, miraculous though it sounds, with the right quantity and quality of spiritual energy, the world could be utterly transformed. Dr King, from whom I learned virtually everything I know about prayer, taught that the only real energy crisis on Earth is the *spiritual* energy crisis, and that until this is put right humankind will always suffer from shortages of more basic forms of energy. Prayer is undoubtedly one of the best ways to help solve this crisis.

"The Angel of Revelation" by William Blake, c.1805.

While I have my own clear ideas about prayer – a subject that is very dear to me – I must stress that this is a book for everyone. All you need is a mind open to the idea that prayer does, or even just might, work, and a willingness to give it a try. We do not have to hold the same beliefs about everything.

My friend and colleague Mark Bennett came up with the following succinct but very timely slogan: "Religions of the world unite, you have nothing to lose but your dogmas!" It should not matter what you call the Divine Source, be it God, Brahma, Allah, Jehovah, Great White Spirit, The Way, Heaven, or anything else. The love in your heart is infinitely more important than the creed in your mind. Prayer is not for the chosen few; it is for everyone. It is the birthright of people of all faiths—and even of none—to experience the benefits that real prayer can bring.

We can all help to improve the world and our own lives this very moment, by being a channel for the limitless energy of love, whether this be manifested in thought, word, deed—or prayer.

And you won't know how good this really is until you try it!

PART ONE

experiencing the energy of prayer

*L*ate one night I was lying in bed, having just finished my regular period of contemplation, and my thoughts wandered as I began to drift off to sleep.

Then, weird though it sounds, even to me, I found myself becoming acutely aware of green, and not a dreamy green but a lively, all-encompassing green, a green radiance —a kind of light—filling my bedroom as if from nowhere, making me feel relaxed but also strangely alert.

After the initial surprise, and slight confusion, at this unfamiliar phenomenon, I began to let go. I knew nothing bad was happening. Twenty years of spiritual practices had taught me the basic difference between the good and the bad as far as mystic states are concerned—I knew nothing sinister was going on. Green is, of course, the color of balance, and as I lay there, lightly contemplating the reason for this strange happening, it all began to make sense.

And why did it make sense? Because thoughts are things.

Thoughts are things

everything we ever think affects the world around us as well as our own lives.

Thoughts are not, contrary to general belief, imprisoned in the brain like goldfish in a bowl. The brain is merely the mechanism that receives and translates thought from the great sea of mind in which we live. In this way it is like a radio, which receives radio waves and translates them into sound. And, also like a radio, the brain can be tuned in to different frequencies. Your radio can be tuned to a station that broadcasts the latest gangster rap or Mozart's finest. Similarly, your brain can be attuned to a frequency of mind that is very basic or extremely inspirational.

But the brain is not only like a radio receiver, it is also like a radio transmitter—it can send thought out over a distance. In fact, not only *can* it do this, an active brain *can't* not do it. Every thought floats out of our physical structures into the sea of mind, changing it for better or worse, or neither.

The concept of positive thinking as a way to improve health and happiness is well established. The subconscious mind responds to positive input and we function better. But what is only just beginning to creep from the arcane to the mainstream is the concept that our thoughts actually affect other people as well as ourselves.

People who allow themselves to be swamped by negativity, and as a result seethe with resentment, jealousy and other negative emotions, are not only harming themselves, but, to some degree, everyone they meet—and even those they do not meet. Why? Because they are making themselves a channel for a very low form of mind, and then sending this outwards, often in a worse state than it originally entered their brains.

Now think about the people who somehow manage to stay positive in even the most dire of situations, who are filled with gratitude, determination, kindness, a love of life, and selflessness. Someone who is genuinely like this is great to be around. These people can lift us up, and make the world seem a better place—because with them around, it *is* a better place. We feel good when in the company of such people, not simply because they may intuitively seem to say the right thing, but also because of the way their brains transmit thought—and when someone's brain is attuned to a higher frequency of mind, his or her whole being becomes a channel through which spiritual energy can flow.

Once this is understood, it brings extra responsibility. A malicious, vengeful thought against someone is not a harmless, powerless indulgence—it will actually

Detail from an ivory statue of a Buddha seated in the lotus position. Burmese School, 19th century.

affect them. It probably won't affect them very much, since most of us use just a tiny fraction of the brain's potential. Conversely, and much more importantly, we have the opportunity to help people more than we may realize. By thought alone you can—believe it or not—help those in need.

So what was that mysterious green light and why was it in my bedroom?

A book I had written, *Journey Into Supermind*, had recently been published. It contains an exercise in which readers are invited to visualize green light, and I had spoken about this practice extensively on the radio. I believe that as people began to use the technique, and because I was the one who had taught it to them, I was picking up on the power of all the "green" thoughts being sent into the sea of mind energy. I was not using visualization but I was unconsciously tuning in to those who were, and the result was a very definite manifestation of that color in my room.

POSITIVITY AND PRAYER

the key question, though, is not so much how thought affects people, but rather how we can gain control of our thoughts and thereby help people. How can we become more positive? How can we train ourselves not to send out negative thoughts?

Let's be honest, it isn't always easy. Most of us have allowed our minds to run rampant for a long time and old habits die hard, but making a change within ourselves is far from impossible and worth every second of effort.

Repeating positive affirmations, such as "Every day in every way I am getting better and better and better and better", can have a tremendous effect. Note that affirmations should always be true—never say an affirmation that is a lie, since this could actually do you more harm than good by prompting the unconscious to prove to you that what you are saying is untrue.

Detail from "Summer Reverie by the Lotus Pond" by Qiu Ying, 16th century—a peaceful scene of relaxation.

Yoga breathing is an excellent way to raise the attunement level of our thinking. The simple technique described on page 56 will give you a flavor of just how potent this practice can be.

And of course, if we think of prayer as communion with the Divine, what could be a better way to raise our thinking to a higher level? If you are good at praying—and all it takes is a bit of practice—your whole life will be scented with prayer's sacred fragrance, and you will become more and more positive in your everyday life.

The more positive you are, the better will be your praying, and the better your praying, the more positive you will be.

in the life of everyone on the spiritual path, no doubt—as in mine—instances, big and small, of the reality of the power of thought are countless. In fact, so innumerable are they, and so natural, that they become just part of living.

Tuning in to the pattern of mind emanations of a person you meet for the first time becomes as automatic as shaking hands and saying "Hello". I'm not saying that you know every detail about them, or could give an instant psychic reading,

Detail from "Abraham and the Angels", a mosaic illustrating the angels' hospitality.

but simply that you have a heightened awareness of the kind of thought, and energy, they radiate. Similarly, since all matter becomes imbued with the thought radiations of the people who come into contact with it, you can quite easily tune in to the "vibe" of a place you may know nothing about and have never been to before.

The practice of psychometry is the psychic science of tuning in to the energy within an object. Contained in the space between particles is the psychic imprint of those people who have come into contact with the object. So, for example, if a psychic takes a ring that you wear every day, he or she will be able to access certain information that you have unconsciously fed into it. If this sounds a little far-fetched, all I can do is recommend that you try it. I have conducted workshops where people who have never done this kind of thing before have held a stranger's ring or watch and been amazed at just how accurate the impressions are that they receive.

Other psychic techniques, such as telepathy, also illustrate the unrestricted movement of thought. One little case that sticks in my mind occurred when I asked a group to pair up with someone else in the class whom they didn't know and take turns to think of an object. The other person had to see if he or she could pick up that thought. I advised them to think of something not too obscure, since it was the first time most of them had ever done this, and I didn't want it to be too difficult. However, one of my students decided to ignore this advice completely, and made the focus of his concentration a sycamore tree. Remarkably, his partner got it absolutely right. These two had never practiced telepathy before—in fact, both of them thought they couldn't do it. There had been no discussion of sycamore or any other trees, and there were none present in the hotel suite where this workshop was held. And yet, out of the blue, one student was able to pick up from the other this virtually unguessable thought.

While such things tell us a bit about how the mind works, which is vital to our understanding of prayer, it is important to remember that prayer has so much more potential. It is a way of directing thought in a powerfully *spiritual* way. The realization that thoughts are transferable cannot but change our whole approach to life—and this change can best be expressed through prayer. No longer are we simply physical beings trapped in bodies, dependent upon limbs and senses to achieve even the simplest of tasks—we are psychic, spiritual beings with a power we never knew we had.

'All that we are is the result of what we have thought: it is founded on our thoughts, it is made up of our thoughts. If a man speaks or acts with a pure thought, happiness follows him, like a shadow that never leaves him.'

Words of the Lord Buddha according to The Dhammapada, *verse 2*

"*Hit him! Hit him! Hit him! Hit him …*"

The sinister chant was deafening. I was trying not to feel afraid, or, at least, not to show it. The whole class of about forty teenaged boys was against me—more for sport than a genuine desire to hurt me, I suppose, but that was of little comfort.

It was my first lesson as a music teacher in a tough school in the early seventies. I was just a few years older than my pupils, and no bigger than the infamous "problem child" who was being egged on to hit me—a boy who was later expelled for whacking the deputy head with a cricket bat and setting light to the chemistry teacher's beard!

This was not the time to try out my powers of persuasion. Reason would have been as useless as a sword against a gun. A show of physical strength, with the laws as they were, even had I succeeded in overpowering him, would probably have resulted in my being taken to court. Prayer was my only hope.

Calling on a spiritual exercise I had been taught by Dr King called "The Protective Practice", I faced my adversary, gazing at him with clear eyes, and, with the purest love I could muster, I silently blessed him. Despite the potentially dangerous situation, slowly, steadily, and very, very gently, I could feel the mysterious light of the Divine Source flowing through me. The threatening stare, scarring his rough features with futile aggression, melted into tacit submission. The sinister chant faded into silence and the music lesson began.

What is love?

"Love" is a word used in many different ways. It can refer to the relationship between parent and child, friends, husband and wife, owner and pet. It can refer to sex. It can even refer to the relationship someone has with an object, as in: "I really love my car."

But real love is not limited to any of these things.

Love between people is complex—much of it is good, but not all. For example, the love that spurs the protective instinct a mother feels for her baby can be wonderful, but the kind of love that leads to jealousy and possessiveness can be destructive. Any kind of love that depends on selfish desire isn't love at all—not real love, in its higher sense. The love that we should strive to manifest in prayer couldn't be more different from selfish desire.

Real love is not a measure of emotion, but something much greater. Being able to channel the extraordinary power of love brings freedom from hate and from a host of other ills. Love can even bring freedom from war, disease, and our own basic selves. Rather than thinking of it as a state of mind, think of it as a state of whole being.

When it says in the Bible: "Love your enemies, bless them that curse you, do good to them that hate you, and pray for them which despitefully use you, and persecute you" (Matthew 5:44), it doesn't, in my view, mean that we necessarily have to *like* our enemies, or people who curse us, hate us, despitefully use us or persecute us. It doesn't mean we have to socialize with them, or buy them Christmas presents. It's not that kind of love at all but rather, an impersonal love in the sense of desiring the highest good for them, ultimately their enlightenment. After all, if they were enlightened, they wouldn't curse us, hate us, despitefully use us or persecute us. One of the ways of putting this love into practical action is by praying that they be inspired to become the people they could be.

Think of hate as fire and love as water. Just as you can't successfully fight fire with fire, nor can you successfully fight hate with hate. The water of love can extinguish the fire of hate—nothing else. Your prayers can be the fountain from which that water flows. This may sound like wishful thinking, but it really is true—with experience you will discover this for yourself. But love is much more than a way to extinguish hate. It is a force for healing, inspiration, and transmutation. Just as life as we know it on Earth could not exist without water, nothing in the universe could exist without love.

All this may seem like a pipe-dream. If the true nature of something all-pervasive is so wonderful, how come everything here on Earth isn't also wonderful? Well, it could be wonderful but it's up to us to make it so, to realize the potential and manifest perfection, by using love in its higher aspects.

RIGHT: *Detail from "Mandala of Amoghapasa", showing the Buddha in meditation. Nepalese school, 19th century.*

This is a simple way of sending energy to those in need.

1. Stand or sit quietly for a few moments with your back as straight as is comfortable, breathing deeply and evenly, with your eyes closed.
Then raise your hands so they are roughly parallel with the top of your shoulders, palms facing outwards, fingers together.

2. Visualize a scintillating white light coming down from above you into your head, charging every cell of the brain with its vibrant power. Take this energy down through your neck and shoulders, on through the chest and out to the front of the heart chakra, a few inches in front of the breastbone. Charge this center with the bright, white light.

3. Then visualize the light coming from the shoulders down through the arms and into the hands. Now direct this energy outwards, so you have a stream of healing white light flowing out from your palms and heart chakra. You are now ready to say your prayer, which is normally done out loud. You can direct the energy wherever you choose, whether it be to a person who is ill or to a region in crisis, visualizing the person or the region not as they are, but as they could be – glowing with spiritual happiness and wellbeing.

4. When you have finished, brush your right hand over your left, away from you. This acts as a seal for the energy and is symbolic of completion of the practice. These hand positions are known in the east as *mudras*, a word particularly associated with Tibet.

Even without mention of a Divine Source, this technique will still have some power, but I would strongly recommend that a request *is* made of the Divine Source – whatever you like to call it. This can help to raise the prayer's energy and empower it by the conscious recognition of the truth that the energy we are using comes from a source greater than ourselves.

Likewise, it is a good thing to end a prayer with a few words of thanks to the Divine Source. Our thanks are not needed, of course, but since we have received something, expending some energy in thanks acts as a token repayment, giving a certain balance to the ritual being performed. Thankfulness also acts as a positive affirmation that a prayer will be effective —otherwise there would be nothing to be thankful for. This confidence in your ability, providing it is not presumptuous, serves to empower the prayer.

Another reason to offer thanks is that it is a way of saying "This is over", helping you to detach from the action, which you should always do rather than worrying about your prayer's effectiveness. Such concern, despite being well intentioned, can interfere with the uplifting energy you have sent out, since all our thoughts produce mental energy, and the mental energy of doubt is counterproductive.

OPPOSITE ABOVE: *Detail from "The Buddha of the Great Miracle". The hand gesture indicates fearlessness. Paitava Monastery, 3rd/4th centuries.* RIGHT: *Detail from "Christ's Ascension" by Giotto, 1303.*

What to pray for?

the answer
to this question might seem obvious to
some people—"For whatever I want!" They would be wrong. As my wife,
Alyson, puts it: "You can get what you want, but do you want what you get?"
We should not pray for whatever we want because whatever we want is not
always good for us.

Spiritual growth, and the happiness that comes with it, is not the result of
satisfying the basic desires we have at present, but of training ourselves to
focus on those desires that are spiritual in nature. With this approach, our
more basic desires will gradually be transmuted into something higher—a
purer expression of love. Easier said than done!

To do something wrong in the physical world is one thing, but to do
something wrong through an invocation of the subtle forces of nature is quite
another. This is known as black magic—using the sea of mind energy for
harmful purposes.

TYPES OF PRAYER TO AVOID INCLUDE:

❖ *Any selfish or materialistic prayer, e.g., praying that you, or even your best friend, win the lottery so as to be able to afford a new Ferrari.*
❖ *Any prayer that affects someone else's free will, e.g., praying that someone falls in love with you, or that someone changes their political views to concord with your own.*
❖ *Any prayer that causes someone else harm. This is not limited to a black-magic rite, e.g., requesting that something bad happen to someone, but refers to any prayer that gives you something by denying it to another person, who may need or deserve it more. For example, it could be wrong to pray for promotion at work, if someone else is more deserving.*

POSITIVE PRAYERS INCLUDE:

❖ *Praying for world peace and freedom.*
❖ *Praying for people engaged in spiritual work, e.g., genuine spiritual teachers, healers, aid workers, fire officers, and others doing similar jobs.*
❖ *Praying for the victims of catastrophes.*
❖ *Praying for yourself or someone else to be healed or inspired.*
❖ *Praying for something that is really needed to achieve a spiritual goal. For example, if you are running a hospital and you know that you need a certain amount of money or else the hospital will close and patients will suffer, this could be a legitimate use for prayer. Even though what you are praying for is materialistic, the motive is not materialistic at all, and that's what counts.*

Whether our prayers are good or bad, the energy used is always the same—the universal life force. The motive behind the prayer, the feeling that conditions it, determines whether the prayer is an act of white magic, black magic, or gray magic, which is somewhere between the two. For our own good, and for the good of others, we should always make our prayers whiter than white.

One way to ensure that your prayers do not inadvertently stray into gray or black magic is to request that whatever it is you are asking for happens *providing it is God's will*. "God's will", which seems a rather vague, old-fashioned term, is a way of saying "for the ultimate good of all life" and you could use these words instead in your prayer, if you prefer.

When sending out energy in a cause such as world peace and freedom, you should not pray for anyone's mind to be changed to a specific point of view. You should pray for people to be so inspired as to seek within, and find the courage and strength to listen to and follow the counsel of their higher selves, their own divine natures. You are sending them energy that they can use, if they consciously or, more likely, unconsciously decide to do so, to inspire *themselves* into doing what is right. In this way, the prayer is not trying to control anyone, but rather to free people from their own limitations and enable them to express their own spiritual motivations.

Enough theory—it's time for a prayer, and why not start with one of the best? "The New Lord's Prayer" is one of my favorites, and is a beautiful example of white magic, which I strongly recommend you to use.

Try saying this prayer as you perform the visualization technique described on page 26. Notice how truly open-hearted the words are—a soulful plea for others to be guided and healed. Balancing this, towards the end, is a request

THE NEW LORD'S PRAYER

Oh Divine and Wondrous Spirit!
Oh Everlasting Lord of Hosts!
Send forth, now, through me
Thy great and lasting Power.

Allow me, oh mighty God, the lasting
   privilege,
Of radiating to all the world Thy great
   Love,
So that those who suffer may be given the
Power and energy to rise above their
   weaknesses.

Oh mighty God, in great humility do I
   ask you
To send forth Your Power.
To give to me this great lasting privilege,
Of being a channel so that my suffering
   brothers
May be helped and guided and healed
   and
Lifted into Thy Light.

So that they who know not may look
   up,
And in doing so, receive through their
   Higher Selves,
Your Divine Counsel.

Oh mighty God, this day have you
   granted me,
A Divine privilege.
I ask you, now, to give to me the
   strength,
So that never again will I turn from my
   inner vision of you;
Om Shanti, Shanti, Shanti.

In praise of your Greatness, oh God,
Doth my Soul sing.
Grant it energy to sing on
Forever and forever.

*Channelled by the Master Jesus
through Dr George King in 1961*

for the person praying to receive strength and inspiration. Make the way you
say this prayer match the words themselves—really allow yourself to express
the power and feeling in every line.

Say it with feeling

for prayer to work properly, it should be expressed with sincerity and feeling, and the whole act should be performed with single-minded concentration. We should not pray as though talking at a coffee afternoon or gossiping with a friend. Prayer is not a telephone call to your mother, or a request made to the boss, a priest, movie star, politician, or even a president—it is an appeal to the Divine Source. Imagine, metaphorically speaking, that you had the opportunity to have an audience with God, if that's how you want to refer to the Divine Source, and say what it is you want and how you feel—this is virtually what is happening when you pray. If you mumble your prayers, or say them without feeling, you are as good as saying, "I don't have to make any effort when expressing myself to God." In fact, this shows a lack of appreciation for the Divine Source of all creation, and therefore for the most important part of yourself, and will considerably limit the power of the prayer.

Jane Austen said: "Grant us grace, almighty Father, so to pray as to deserve to be heard." She made a good point. Technically, all prayers "deserve to be heard", because they invoke and transmit a certain amount of energy, but the quantity and quality of the energy will increase dramatically when we start to pray dynamically.

Try saying "The New Lord's Prayer", or indeed any other white-magic prayer, in as expressive a manner as you can. Don't worry about seeming silly. Just give it all you've got. Make it as dynamic in intensity, but not volume, as a scream you might let out if someone ran over your foot, and as wholehearted as when a football fan cheers for his or her favorite team, although exerting more self-control. You don't have to be very loud—the important thing is not to hold back at all. Imagine that your very life depends on every single word. Don't be melodramatic or over-emotional. Put genuine feeling and love into it. This is the first step.

CONTROLLING PRAYER ENERGY

the next step—when you've got used to saying a prayer out loud with all the feeling you can muster, thus invoking and transmitting much more energy than you did before—is to train yourself to gain more control over the energy. This will enable you to act as a channel for even more, and better quality, energy, which will, in turn, make your prayers better than ever.

Prayer should be a balanced symphony of opposites, a melody of yin and yang, a harmonious blend of light and shade, each bringing the other to life. To gain more control over prayer energy, you should be:

- *gentle, but also definite and firm*
- *passionate, but controlled and not too emotional*
- *filled with compassion and want the result of the prayer with all your heart, and yet also be detached from it*
- *imploring, yet confident of the outcome of the prayer*
- *humble, and yet feel as powerful as the Divine Source, which is our essence.*

With the development of these qualities, your prayers should become quieter without losing any of the intensity displayed when praying loudly. A good way of cultivating these opposite attributes is to alternate the volume of your prayer a little, so that some words and phrases are louder than others, and some words may be barely audible at all.

Praying like this is not easy and can take a lot of practice. Remember, you are making yourself a channel to *allow* the energy to flow through you. You are not trying to force it. Your body should not be tense to the point of shaking. Instead, you should be physically relaxed, while trying to maintain the posture described in the prayer technique.

Often you may not feel in the mood to pray at all. In fact, when we feel at our lowest, prayer can be a struggle, but this is the very time when praying can do the most good. So try it. Just do one short prayer. My own experience is that this can change your mood so quickly that you may well feel like carrying on and saying more prayers as soon as you've finished the first one.

Prayer and personality go hand in hand. Everyone has an individual way of praying, even when adhering to the same principles, as listed above. What is interesting, though, is that our true personality seems to be revealed by prayer—after all, prayer has to be genuine to mean anything at all. It has to come from the soul. Someone who is apparently very passive might suddenly come to life during prayer, becoming almost unrecognizable. This is that person's real personality. The one he or she usually shows is merely the surface of the still, deep ocean of his or her true spiritual nature.

Learning to pray is not just the acquisition of an incredibly useful, practical skill. It is a tool for personal transformation and discovery. As your ability improves, you will find that you improve throughout your life in countless different ways. It will, in short, bring out the very best in you.

Detail from "Coronation of the Virgin" by Carlo Crivelli, 1478.

Where to pray

in some ways, it doesn't really matter where you pray. The most important things are knowing what to pray for and then to go on and do it, and in the right way, as previously described.

Where to pray comes way down the pecking order, after these three key requirements are met, but, nevertheless, it is an aspect of spiritual knowledge that every prayerful soul should consider. Sometimes, it can make all the difference—praying in a spiritually powerful place, for instance, can be tremendously uplifting and inspirational.

We can pray anywhere—and should pray almost everywhere. What I mean by this is not that we should raise our hands and burst into dynamic prayer in the middle of the office or supermarket, or in a bar, or at the beauty salon, but that we should try to keep the Divine Source in our minds as much as we can, without neglecting other essential duties. One of the things I respect about Islam is the fact that serious adherents are expected to pray at five set

LEFT: *Detail from "A Multitude of Seated Buddhas", from interior of a cave. Indian School, 5th century.*

Detail from "Richard II Adoring the Madonna". French School, c.1395.

times throughout the day—*every single day*. In some parts of the Muslim world, everything stops at these times, and everyone unites in prayer. This may seem extreme to our western, secular culture, but it is undeniably an excellent way of keeping God in a prominent position in minds and hearts.

As well as trying to think about God throughout the day, we should also think about compassion. For example, next time you see an ambulance, spare a silent prayer for the person in need, and for those trying to help that person, visualizing the vehicle being filled with healing white light. Naturally you should not allow this to distract you from driving or stepping out of the way of the ambulance as it approaches, but it is rare for our minds to be so occupied, and our concentration so under pressure, that we cannot spare a fleeting thought of compassion at times like these—and every thought helps. Your one fleeting thought could be just what someone needed at that second—not pity, or regret, but real, active, detached, vibrant compassion.

Aside from incidents such as these, when we want to pray properly, to surrender to the love coursing through us, we need to choose a place where we feel comfortable. This can be indoors or outdoors—in our own home or in a building we have never been to before. There are no rules for this kind of thing— just ideas. Personally, I find one of the most inspirational places to pray is on a high hill or mountain, especially one known to be holy. In the Aetherius Society, we make pilgrimages to nineteen New Age holy mountains around the world:

Africa
Mount Kilimanjaro, Tanzania

Australia
Mount Kosciusko, New South Wales
Mount Ramshead, New South Wales

Europe
Mount Mederger Flue, Switzerland
Le Nid D'Aigle, France

Great Britain
Holdstone Down, Devon, England
Brown Willy, Cornwall, England
Ben Hope, The Highlands, Scotland
Creag-An-Leth-Chain, Grampian, Scotland

The Old Man Of Coniston, Cumbria, England
Pen-Y-Fan, Powys, Wales
Carnedd Llywelyn, Gwynedd, Wales
Kinderscout, Derbyshire, England
Yes Tor, Devon, England

New Zealand
Mount Wakefield, South Island

USA
Mount Baldy, Southern California
Mount Tallac, Lake Tahoe, Northern California
Mount Adams, New Hampshire
Castle Peak, Aspen, Colorado

Anyone who has felt the colossal spirituality held within these mountains can have no doubt about their sacred power. When we allow ourselves to be channels, not just for the light of God from above, but for the energies in the ground beneath our feet, prayer can take on a whole new dimension.

The potency of the mountains—and of prayer itself—was illustrated to me in a way that nobody, including me, expected, shortly after I had begun work on this book. I was privileged to be leading a pilgrimage, marking an anniversary, to Holdstone Down in Devon on Saturday, July 26 2008, where 135 people gathered to send spiritual energy not to friends, family, or each other, or even to the world as a whole, but, instead, to the "Great Ones", for want of a better term—to the Masters who watch over us in largely silent, but ever-patient, compassion; to the Gods who have been our guides and saviors for millennia.

All those who took part believe that these Gods come from other planets. Having worked in this field now for over thirty years, I have no doubt whatsoever that ours is but one planet among many that teem with life – and, in terms of the people who live here, not even a very advanced one.

Just hours after we had sent energy, through prayer, to these great beings, there were, unbeknown to us until a few days later, a record of over 200—yes, 200—sightings of UFOs seen by people all over the UK!

Surely even the most conditioned of cynics couldn't help but wonder at the synchronicity of such a happening. To the believer, and the open-minded seeker, here you have a truly inspirational glimpse of what a few can do. It is said that for every step we take toward the Great Ones, they take two toward us—not an empty promise or idle words designed to comfort or please, but a simple truth. And this truth is illustrated, in myriad ways, to everyone who has ever, in their hearts, minds, and, crucially, in their actions, taken such a step.

However, we cannot all afford the time and energy to travel hundreds of miles to our nearest holy mountain every time we want to pray, and, much as we might like to, we cannot all live near such a place. Some of us are in a better position to offer service amid the clatter of a city or a town.

CREATING A SANCTUARY AT HOME

we can all create a prayer sanctuary in our own homes. A quiet spare room is just right for the purpose but otherwise try to find a corner, or some other out-of-the-way area, that you can devote solely to spiritual practices. Ideally, you would face the east for this, but it is not essential.

It doesn't have to be a large space or decorated in any special way—just a clean and pleasant spot where you feel at ease. The elaborate decorations of certain temples and churches, while great feats of artistic skill and imagination, are not necessarily conducive to spiritual practice. For prayer, and especially for meditation, simple is often best. The energy of such complexity, while uplifting sometimes, can also be a distraction from the task at hand.

Detail of the Buddha seated in lotus position. Gilt bronze statue.

That is not to say that we should feel obliged to be overly puritanical. Pictures and objects that have spiritual significance can help in a place of prayer. Rather than acting as a distraction, they can help us to focus and detach from the secular world. The choice of such items will depend on personal preference and cultural background. The difference between the efficacy of a Christian rosary and a Buddhist mandala cannot be quantified into a general rule.

One piece of advice I would give, though, is to avoid any kind of negative images, even if they originate from a sound spiritual tradition. The gargoyles and blood-stained crucifixes of many cathedrals, the monstrous-looking Yama of the underworld in folk Buddhism, and the explicit symbolism of some tantric images, are not recommended for a prayer sanctuary. Pick something unambiguously pure—such as Raphael's painting of the *Ascension of Christ*, or a photograph of a wise-eyed Indian Swami, such as Sri Ramakrishna, or Swamis Sivananda or Vivekananda. Items such as these will help you to attune to the higher things in life. The devotee of a great sage, saint, Master, or avatar can virtually bring the presence of such a spiritual giant into the sanctuary.

❖ *Use the physical senses to lift your mind toward the spirit through color, sound, and smell. A mid-spectrum green lightbulb will imbue your sacred space with a balancing, healing light, which is ideal for spiritual practice.*
❖ *Select suitable music to play before you commence your prayers, such as choral plainsong or certain types of New Age music. Placid classical music without too much rhythmic or melodic content can also be appropriate—something from the Baroque tradition, for example. Too strong a melody can distract the mind; it may be great art but may not necessarily create the atmosphere you want. Likewise, a strong rhythm can have a distracting mental or even physical effect upon you.*
❖ *Finally, set out scented candles or flower oils as used in aromatherapy, or you may prefer the more traditional incense from sandalwood, or another perfume associated with meditative or religious activities.*

Your sacred place, if used properly and regularly, will become a real haven for you. When the world seems bleak and godless, as it will to all seekers at times, go to this sanctuary and raise your hands in prayer. Although this may not be the solution to all your problems, you will feel better—and, however oppressive the darkness may seem, a glimmer of light will shine brightly enough to guide you through the stormy seas of the transient illusions of what ancient Sanskrit writings refer to as "maya" (materialistic delusion).

Association plays a part in this—simply seeing your sacred space will lift you up to a degree—but the reason for having a sanctuary is much more than psychological. As you may recall from the section on page 15, "Thoughts are things", we are biological transmitting machines. We radiate thoughts and energy that impress and change the people and things around us whether we are aware of this or not. Your sanctuary will become imbued by your delicate, subtle, healing radiations as your soul sings in praise of the Divine and in heart-centered yearning for the end of suffering for all life.

Try to visit a place of worship that is conducive to your spiritual practice, where you can join with others in prayer, be it temple, church, mosque, or synagogue. The important thing is whether it is a good place for you to radiate pure spiritual light and love whenever you are able to attend it.

At the time of writing this book, the Aetherius Society is in the process of converting a large building in Fulham, southwest London, into a temple where members and friends can meet to worship. We will practice a combination of New Age Christian prayer, ancient Buddhist and Hindu mantras, and a number of visualization techniques for the betterment of the world and the spiritual upliftment of the congregation. It will be open to any member of the public who wishes to join us.

The very fact that hundreds will come to such a place for such a motive will add to its power. We envisage it becoming a place of light in the midst of a busy city, which is focused, as all cities are, mainly on materialistic acquisition and pleasure, albeit with is own unique cultural and intellectual tradition. Such an oasis of spirituality in a place that can be anything from frenetic to mundane but could hardly ever be described as soulful, will be not only a refuge but a transmuting force for love, peace, and divinity.

A bright cigar-shaped object glided through the night sky. It had been on the news—apparently, hundreds of people had seen it. But to hear about something on the news and to see it for yourself are two very different things. Here it was, before our very eyes. My friend John and I—both students at the time—got out of our battered old Austin, walked briskly across the damp field in front of us, all the while gazing at the strange object, which I believe was a celestial vehicle from another planet, as it moved silently through the starlit heavens above us.

Then, to our disappointment, it became obscured by a large oak tree. Under the oak tree was a brand-new pair of gym shoes, and an aspect of karma became clear to me ...

Detail of a seated Buddha in meditation. Statue, 1st/4th century.

Karma

to understand the efficacy of prayer, it is essential to have an understanding of the basic principles of karma. In the Bible it says: "... whatsoever a man soweth, that shall he also reap" (Galatians 6:7), which describes karma simply, but perfectly. "Action and reaction are opposite and equal" stated Newton in his third law of motion, doubtless unaware that his maxim would be used by posterity to describe the Buddha's teachings on karma. "What goes around, comes around" is perhaps the most mundane description of karma—as recently popularized in a song of the same name. In fact, the idea of karma is no stranger to pop culture. It was also the theme of John Lennon's song "Instant Karma" and the subject of the hit TV comedy *My Name is Earl*. Although these things are comparatively trivial, their popularity may be indicative of humankind's innate awareness that karma is the musical structure within which the song of life is composed.

What is unfortunate is that, despite this popularity, karma is seldom understood, which can occasionally lead to simplistic interpretations that are little better than primitive notions of eternal damnation. If we tend to view life as a learning process rather than a test, and karma as our teacher rather than our punisher, we can't go far wrong. Spiritual evolution comes as a result of gaining mastery over the challenges of life, and to achieve this we need to go through both pleasant and unpleasant experiences. Exactly when and why a particular experience is presented to us is not always easy to see. It is certainly not necessarily the case, for example, that a rich man is more spiritually advanced than a poor one, or that a healthy man is more evolved than an unhealthy one. An advanced person may need to go through very difficult experiences in order to learn lessons and rise even higher up the ladder of evolution.

Prayer should not be viewed as useless in the face of so-called "bad" karma, but nor should karma be forgotten when thinking about prayer. When you transmit spiritual energy to people in need, what you are actually doing is sending them energy that they can use to overcome their karmic difficulties and move forward. You are not transmuting their negative karma for them—you are helping them to transmute their own negative karma. By doing this, you are creating good karma for yourself, because every time you send out energy, by karmic law, you receive energy back, although not necessarily immediately. This creates an expanding spiral—the more spiritual energy you send out, the more you receive, and the more you receive, the more you are able to send out.

RECEIVING WHAT YOU SACRIFICE

through karma, not only do you receive what you give—whether it be energy through prayer or anything else—but you also receive what you sacrifice. If, for example, you are a true

RIGHT: *"The Mystic Circle of Phyag-rdor and the Eight Serpent Divinities". Mandala Vajrapani, c.1849.*

humanitarian, who also has a great interest in meditation, and what you would really like to do is go off to an ashram and spend most of the day sitting cross-legged in search of the shining light of wisdom within, but you decide not to do that and instead resolve to devote yourself to helping others here and now, then you are making a sacrifice. You are giving up spiritual attainment for the sake of something greater. The karmic result of this will be that, at some point in the future, at the right time, you will be given the opportunity to achieve the very same spiritual attainment that you sought, and not only this. By sacrifice, you will have woven the correct karmic magic to empower the whole process. Your spiritual progress will be surer, more lasting, and more inspired than ever it could have been had you simply opted to go for a life of lengthy meditation, ignoring the needs of others.

Gilded statue of Buddha from Ananda Temple in Burma.

An example of this karmic principle—that "what you give up is laid at your feet"—was illustrated to me in a very literal way by the UFO story with which this chapter begins. As if having the privilege of such a good sighting wasn't amazing enough, those clean, fresh, unworn shoes—apparently unremarkable in every way—were, for me, very significant. Just a few days earlier, I had had to make a choice between buying a new pair of gym shoes or some Aetherius Society books and cassettes on spiritual truth relating to UFOs and those who manned them. I had decided to go without the gym shoes and get the books and cassettes. Then the very thing that I had foregone, small though it was, was laid at my feet—as it happened, for my feet! Do I think the UFO had put the shoes there? No, of course not. I didn't interpret what had happened as some kind of sensationalist out-of-this-world miracle. It was, to me, first and foremost, simply a sign. The "coincidence" of it all, or, since there is no such thing as coincidence, the synchronicity, was extraordinary.

I am not for one minute saying that you have to believe in this story to believe in karma. But it does show that sacrifice for the right reason (even a small sacrifice such as this) is rewarded.

Sacrifice, when it is called for, is a kind of liberation—it frees you from the false, the unnecessary, or the less important, and enables you to do, and be, something amazing. It is the sword that cuts you from the shackles of attachment, so that you can rise higher and higher through evolution. It is the very essence of the impersonal love that was discussed earlier on.

In prayer, we should develop a sense of sacrifice—as we give the whole of ourselves to the prayer, we are virtually sacrificing all that we are for that moment of love in action. We are sacrificing our time, our concentration, and our energy for a higher purpose. Thinking about this principle, and then actively cultivating it within ourselves, will empower our prayers from a karmic point of view—and raise their quality to a vastly higher level.

Forgiveness

karma cannot bestow "forgiveness" upon any of us, regardless of who we are or what we believe. So-called negative karma must be transmuted by doing good. Karma cannot just "let us off" when we do something contrary to divine law, because if it did we would not learn the essential lessons.

I do not believe that by joining any particular religion our karmic slate is wiped clean, and we should not want this to be the case. It would mean missing the experiences that we require, and with which karma invariably provides us, to evolve and eventually return to the Divine Source, finally fully conscious of our own divinity.

So I don't believe in praying to a Divine Source for the forgiveness of our sins. But I do believe prayer can be used to confess our faults and failings so that in this spirit of honesty before God we can resolve to overcome them and be strengthened in this purpose.

The word "forgiveness" has two basic meanings—to cease to feel resentful toward someone, and to let someone off instead of taking action against them. The distinction between these two meanings is crucial.

We should forgive everyone for every wrong done to us, in the sense of freeing ourselves from resentment, but not necessarily in the sense of doing nothing about the wrong in question. Resentment is a source of great pain—certainly to the person harboring it, and often to others too, if allowed to fester. It serves no useful purpose and is a hindrance to our spiritual development. You may well need to do something about rectifying the wrong done to you, but not from a standpoint of resentment so much as one of being truthful and doing the right thing.

Prayer is a great way to help us forgive other people. Not only can we pray for the strength, courage, and magnanimity to forgive, we can also pray for guidance on whether or not to take action over the wrong in question, and what action to take. More than this, we can send streams of vibrant white light—of love—to anyone against whom we may be harbouring resentment. In this way, we can transmute the negative thought pattern we have created within ourselves, and also the bad vibes we have sent to this person. In addition, by directing inspiring light energy their way, we can help him or her to become a better person, who is less likely to commit a similar wrong in the future.

RIGHT: *Egyptian statue of a praying priest, 21st dynasty, 1080–10.*

Healing

one of the most beneficial practices that anyone can perform is to give healing to others. All that is required is the genuine desire to help, and an extremely effective way of doing it is to use prayer to send healing to others and, indeed, to yourself.

The ability to heal is not a gift bestowed on a chosen few, nor is it subservient to the whim of a strange, capricious deity. It is a skill that can be learned. Results depend on performance, and also on the recipient's situation, including their karmic pattern and conscious or unconscious willingness to accept the energy offered. Needless to say, spiritual healing should be regarded as complementary to other forms of treatment, including conventional medicine, not as a substitute, whether it is used to help oneself, a group, or a single individual.

When sending healing to an individual in need, the key to that person's recovery is that he or she learns whatever lesson or lessons the bout of illness is karmically designed to teach. Then the lesson(s) will no longer be necessary and therefore the illness will, one way or another, disappear.

Always visualize the focal point of your healing in robust health and surrounded by white light. Do not visualize the person with any illness because by doing so you may empower that ill health. By visualizing the person well, you will do the exact opposite and speed up the healing process.

In these critical times of global change, even more important than the healing of individuals is the healing of the whole world. "The New Lord's Prayer" (see page 31) is ideal for this. If you wish, you can specify a particular situation, such as war, famine, or natural disaster, asking for healing to go to the victims of it. Be sure to keep your visualizations positive. See a war-torn area bathed in peace; even though people may be suffering or starving in a particular region, see them healed and relieved from their dire situation.

While healing the world is the noblest goal, healing yourself is also often necessary and is a perfectly valid use of prayer. Again, you should be careful to approach this from a spiritual standpoint. It is good to include in your self-healing prayers an element of karmic awareness—in other words, desire to cure yourself through learning from your present situation and moving onward, rather than just asking straightforwardly to be in better health.

RIGHT: *Detail from "The Raising of Jairus's Daughter". Mosaic, 12th century.*

Yoga and enlightenment

as we learn more about spirituality, we should cultivate that side of ourselves with the aim of entering the deep mystic states that yield wisdom and ultimately lead to enlightenment. Only then can selflessness—which is the axis of all spirituality—blossom into full bloom, because only then do we have the abilities and the understanding to render the most effective possible service to all.

Making ourselves channels for spiritual energy through prayer will

heighten our spiritual awareness and also, slowly but surely, develop and enhance our latent psychic and intuitive abilities, and even lead to mystic states. Prayer can sensitize us in such a way that we become more open to the subtle and higher forces of nature that exist all around us. Performing such spiritual practices as concentration, contemplation, and meditation can have a similar effect and also improve our ability to pray. I would recommend that anyone serious about learning to pray take up yoga breathing, which helps to improve body, mind, psychic ability, and spiritual awareness. The technique that follows, which is taught in traditional schools of yoga, is safe and effective. If practiced correctly and regularly, it will give you a good idea of just how beneficial yogic breathing can be. Another method, the safest and most effective I know, is explained in *Realise Your Inner Potential*, a book I was privileged to co-author with Dr King in the last year of his earthly life.

ABOVE: *Detail of the seated Buddha, making the symbolic sign: "The Preaching of the Golden Middle Way".* LEFT: *Detail of Buddha in a Bodhisattva form.*

1. Sit with your back as straight as possible, either on a hard-backed chair or, if you are supple enough, on the floor cross-legged, or in a suitable yoga posture. Close your eyes. Start to breathe deeply and evenly. You should try to remain alert, yet relaxed. In yoga, the aim is to train your mind, body, and heart into a more spiritual way of life without forcing anything too abruptly.

2. Now, think of the upper part of the body—from the bottom of your trunk to the top of your shoulders—as being like a glass. On the in-breath, visualize this part of yourself being filled with white liquid, or white light. Just as a glass would be filled from the base to the brim, see the bottom of the trunk being filled first, until the white liquid or light reaches the top of your shoulders. Then on the out-breath, see this part of yourself being emptied of the white liquid or light, from the top downwards.

3. It is important to fill the whole of the glass, and also to empty it completely. On the in-breath, your stomach and chest region should swell out, and on the out-breath the abdomen can be pulled inwards.

4. In prayer, we attract universal life force to ourselves and then send it outwards. The principle here is not that different. By the power of visualization, we draw energy—the white liquid or light—into ourselves for our purification, magnetization, and spiritualization.

5. This practice encourages the practitioner to use the whole of the upper part of the body during the breathing process, which has clear physical benefits. Once you become accustomed to breathing more completely, this will tend to continue naturally during both your waking and sleeping states.

when talking about yoga, you can't get very far

without talking about the chakras, sometimes referred to as psychic centers, and the kundalini. Yoga, so much more than a keep-fit regime, is an extremely efficient, potent path to enlightenment, a whole philosophy of being. The word "yoga" means "union", implying "union with the Divine Source", which is, or should be, the goal of all yoga practice, whether it be hatha yoga for health, raja yoga for mental and psychic control, gnani yoga for wisdom, bhakti yoga for love and devotion, or karma yoga for service to others.

The kundalini is a mysterious, immensely powerful, awe-inspiringly sacred psychic force, sometimes called "the serpent power". It lies at the base of the spine, usually coiled like a snake. All our actions are dependent upon the kundalini. We couldn't do anything without this power. Although largely dormant in most people, it is still sufficiently active to enable us to gain the experiences that our own karmic pattern requires of us.

Through yoga, this power rises up the spine, passing through each chakra as it goes. The term "kundalini yoga" is overused and all too often the exercises taught bear very little resemblance to this most powerful system of spiritual development. It is important to discriminate carefully when pursuing this path. Some systems have very little to do with the true practice of kundalini yoga; others are too advanced for the average practitioner and could be dangerous to attempt.

To experience a substantial rise of kundalini is extremely rare. A full rise is even rarer. Most of the kundalini experiences we read about are partial rises, which, although significant, are very different from a full rise.

As the power passes through the chakras, each one in turn becomes activated, giving the aspirant a different set of experiences and psychic powers. When the kundalini can be raised at will to the highest chakra, known as the crown center, "brahma chakra" or, in Sanskrit, "sahasrara", located above the head, then it is said that full mastery has been gained over mortal experience of life on Earth. The aspirant is a Master ready for Ascension, which is when that individual leaves the reincarnation cycle on Earth and goes on to greater experiences and greater forms of service to others.

Understood in this light, we should never underestimate the importance of the kundalini. Command of it gives us mastery over ourselves. In other words, the big question "Why are we here?", which can sometimes seem so arcane as to be almost comical, actually has an answer. We are here to gain control over the kundalini.

Yogic practices exist that focus on raising the kundalini through force. I would not recommend these. The kundalini is a great power and, like all great powers, has to be handled very carefully. A person who is not ready to start forcing the rise of the kundalini, whether it be due to a lack of purity, a lack of concentration, or some other reason, but who attempts to do so without the correct supervision, could end up in severe difficulties, including suffering from mental or physical disability.

The safe way is to coax the kundalini gently up the spine, in a balanced manner, primarily through giving service to others. This is karma yoga and it may seem a very slow method, but it is a very sure one in comparison to the dangerous practices of some of the schools of the East. Karma yoga should be

RIGHT: *Tibetan painted textile, showing the Buddha meditating.*

complemented by certain spiritual practices from other schools of yoga, such as yogic breathing, positive visualizations, and chanting mantras. These things help to prepare body and mind for the full rise of the kundalini in the future.

However, rather than regarding karma yoga as "the low path" for those not considered ready for the higher one, we should think of it as being the greatest of all the yogas. After all, what is greater than helping others? The other yogas, if practiced properly, can yield excellent results, but none of them on their own really grapple with the immediate problems the world is facing.

Traditionally, the idea behind yoga is that we should gain enlightenment, primarily through meditation, and only then are we fit to be of any serious use to the world. While perhaps a valid approach once, this is not the case today. The world is suffering and needs us—now.

We live in an era of potentially dramatic change on many levels—not least climate change, the danger of science rampaging out of control, and the threat of nuclear war. Prayer can certainly help the world in these strange times—in fact, the world may need our prayers like never before—but prayer alone is not enough. We must also *work* for what is right, whether through teaching, aid work, medical assistance, campaigning for justice, or any other course. There is no shortage of work to be done. Similarly, in our own lives, it is not enough to pray for something without lifting a finger to do anything about it. Prayer is but one method of solving problems, sometimes the best, sometimes not—it all depends on the situation.

"By prayer one's subtle powers are easily roused, and if consciously done all desires may be fulfilled by it."

Swami Vivekananda

What is the Divine?

a well-known parable told by the great Hindu sage Sri Ramakrishna recounts how several blind people were taken into the presence of an elephant for the first time. Each of them touched one part of the elephant – one touched the legs, one the trunk, one the belly, one the ears, and so on. Then they each described what the elephant was like, focusing solely on the one part they had felt with their own hands. Their descriptions, naturally, differed considerably, but they were all describing the same thing.

So it is with God, said Sri Ramakrishna. All the great religions—Hinduism, Christianity, Islam, Judaism, Daoism, Buddhism, Shintoism, and Paganism among them—convey different aspects of the Divine. It is only when we accept the merits of these religions as complementary rather than contradictory—and, more importantly, when we make active spirituality an integral part of our lives—that a fuller, less limited approach to the Divine becomes possible.

When we look at the universe and see the specks of cosmic dust that we are, we may examine the intricate wonder of life—from the complexities of the human psyche to the artistry of the ever-changing canvas that is the sky above our heads. Then we can ask what is behind it all, what is its essence?

What is the fundamental thread of logic that ties creation together? What is the essence of *everything*?

Questions such as these begin to dissolve conventional views of an individual, personal creator with likes and dislikes, and gradually instill in us a more fitting sense of the great mystery of creation. By contemplating the vastness of infinity, and the limitlessness of eternity, a better appreciation of the true might of the great unifying principle becomes apparent, and helps us to develop a better understanding of it all, because we start to realize that this unifying principle also unites us to the whole, as a small, but essential part of that whole.

Add to this the perfection of karma as an essential force in evolution, and

Indian miniature of a yogi by a lotus pond, from a series of depictions of yoga practice in Hindu verse, 1760.

the beauty of true divine love, which we can experience through prayer and other means, and the universe immediately becomes entirely different from the place we inhabited prior to this kind of awakening.

This is the dawning of faith—not blind faith, but the vision that enables us to see life, however hard it may be, as the wonderful thing that it is, and that, whatever name you care to use, God is all.

prayer is a way to focus our hearts and

minds on the divine principle. In Hindu and Buddhist traditions, mantras are chanted, using Sanskrit words to point to the divine presence within us all. Although the main power of mantras is created by the sound of these words rather than their literal meaning, one of the effects of this form of prayer is to focus our consciousness on the Divine. Although it is not the remit of this book, I thoroughly recommend mantra yoga, which I practice regularly.

Realization of divinity does not come from rational debate— it is a result of the awakening of that part of ourselves that already knows it is divine. My favorite book title is *How to Know God*, attributed to the aphorisms of the ancient yogi Sri Patanjali. This title suggests that, ultimately, knowledge of God is not based on belief or even faith but is something you can experience.

Prayer is a wonderful way to help bring this about and thereby release us from uncertainty about our unlimited divine potential and the true glory of God as the Absolute— all that which is manifested and all that which is not.

" 'I am naught,' said a man.
'Naught but me,' answered God."

Dr George King

Detail from a 10th century Korean sculpture
of a cross-legged Shakyamuni Buddha.

Heroes of prayer

'Prayer is the ecstasy of the mystic, the meditation of the sage, and the soaring rapture of the saint.'

ANNIE BESANT

the individuals in this section illustrate, above all, that prayer is not the sober tedium that many may associate with reciting a few words on a Sunday morning—it is an adventure in itself, and a path to liberation.

I have picked four people from among the numerous heroes of prayer as examples. They are from different spiritual backgrounds. Paramahansa Yogananda (1893–1952) was a Hindu yogi, Jalal al-Din Rumi (1207–73) was a Sufi—Sufism being the mystical branch of the Islamic tradition—St Teresa of Ávila (1515–82) was a Roman Catholic nun, and Dr George King (1919–97) was a New Age spiritual teacher. It is interesting to note that these heroes of prayer proved themselves to be enthusiasts of the unity of religion, rather than espousing their own as "the one and only way". This is true of them all, except, as far as I am aware, St Teresa, who, in the climate of the infamous Inquisition, probably would have known little of other faiths—and certainly would not have been able publicly to state her sympathies with them if she had. Nevertheless, some of her experiences strike me as being remarkably similar to yogic and mystical feats from other traditions.

The more I think about these individuals, the more I am convinced of their heroism, albeit in far from equal degree. People don't normally associate prayer with heroism, but I would suggest that we should. Heroism doesn't apply exclusively to courage in the heat of battle; nor is it necessarily practiced in a fanfare of publicity. Very often it is silent, still, unnoticed. Sometimes it is not regarded as heroism at all. In fact, I would venture to suggest that a hero with no opposition is no hero at all. For, in this strange world of ours, darkness follows light like the shadow that follows a saint on a summer's day. But when the light shines in all directions from within, the shadow will, eventually, be dispelled and the darkness will be vanquished once and for all.

True heroism involves strength, self-control, impersonal love, and selflessness. True prayer not only embodies such qualities but is one of the most undiluted expressions of the higher attributes of the human psyche that it is possible to display on a daily basis. Our prayers can, quite literally, save lives and even help to save the world. What could be more heroic than that?

Eyes of the god Horus, painted to ward off evil. The left eye symbolizes the moon, the right eye the sun. Egyptian, 12th dynasty.

A long-haired Indian yogi prays alone in his room in an ashram. If you could feel the intensity of his silent plea, there would be no doubt in your mind about the sheer profundity of his sincerity. Here was a Hindu intent with all his heart and soul on shedding light on the New Testament of the Christian Bible. He longed for the great Jesus himself to illuminate the true meaning of the words, which had been obscured and shrouded in mystery for so long, so that he would be able to spread this wisdom to others thirsting for sacred truth.

The combination of perseverance, purity, and wholehearted spiritual desire brought a miraculous and most treasured reward. We are told that the room filled with a blue light and the magnificent, youthful, radiant form of Jesus appeared before him and spoke …

Detail from an Indian miniature, showing an ascetic meditating in his garden.

an experience such as this is rare to say the least, but it illustrates an important lesson – that by truly following the spiritual path, all manner of miracles are possible. When no result is forthcoming, it is due to lack of effort, not an absence of divinity, for divinity is ever-present. The above incident did not take place thousands of years ago up a mountain in the Himalayas. It happened in the middle of the last century in one of the most worldly of all corners of the globe – California.

Yogananda was born in 1893 to a devout, well-to-do family in northeast India. His father held a senior position in a large railway company, and was inclined towards maths and logic. His mother was a sensitive, kindly woman, whose extravagant generosity to the needy caused her practical husband serious concern. It is not hard to see in their son a higher synthesis of these two very different, but complementary, personalities. The story of his life and of the lives of many other saints and sages, recounted so beautifully in his classic *Autobiography of a Yogi*, have inspired generations of spiritual seekers. The romantic, devotional

"The Ascension" by William Blake, c.1805–6.

style of his writing cannot veil the immense practical skill and dogged determination demonstrated by such a pioneer, one of the first Indian spiritual teachers to live permanently in the west. His goal was to share the yogic wisdom that had been given to him by his Master, Sri Yukteswar, with seekers to whom this tradition was almost entirely alien.

His mission, however, was a far cry from that of nineteenth-century western missionaries whose reputation for great courage in trekking through Africa is tarnished by what was often a disturbingly dogmatic approach. While such missionaries may have been well intentioned, an all-too-frequent attitude of "I'm completely right and you're completely wrong" was indicative of a spiritual immaturity that has no place in the modern world. Yogananda's commitment to his native Hindu faith was unshakable but this didn't make him dogmatic; on the contrary, it gave him the wisdom to see the unity of religion – the fundamental threads of compassion and visions of higher reality expressed in different ways by different people at different times.

He was still only in his late twenties when he received an invitation to speak at the International Congress of Religious Liberals, which was to take place in Boston in October 1920. The invitation did not come as a surprise. The day before, while in meditation, he had had a vision, which he had correctly interpreted as meaning that he was being called from his native India to the distant, utterly foreign land of America. Excited, but at the same time sad at leaving behind so much of what he loved, he was also somewhat perturbed by the prospect of giving lectures in English – something he had never done before. Another problem was the need to find the requisite

LEFT: *Detail from a miniature painting of a yogini in a landscape setting.*

finance, which he sought from his extremely reluctant father, whose initially stern refusal melted into generous support the following day.

But these concerns were petty in comparison with the much more serious issue of his spiritual welfare. After all, it is one thing to be a devout yogi in India, immersed in a tradition that values and understands such a way of life, surrounded by supportive, like-minded spiritual aspirants, but it is quite another to venture to a foreign land, regarded as notoriously materialistic by the average high-minded yogi, and to maintain the selfsame zeal of faith, devotion, and practice. Then, as well as needing to cultivate this zeal to such an extent that the harvest of dedication would be bountiful enough to feed himself, this harvest would also need to feed the multitude of spiritually malnourished seekers whom it was his goal to serve.

Early one morning, prior to his voyage, Yogananda began to pray with a degree of unyielding ardor rare even for him. He resolved to carry on praying, even to the point of death, until he heard the Lord's reassurance that his soul would not drown in the shallows of western materialism. After hours of fervent pleading, so we are told, there was a knock at the door and in walked a yogi, dressed in the meager attire of a renunciant. The Master before him—who was, and is, of literally otherworldly spiritual caliber—gave him the peace of mind he had been seeking, and also scattered other seeds of wisdom in Yogananda's fertile mind. This Master was none other than the Lord Babaji, who is regarded as the most elevated of all the Masters on Earth.

Yogananda founded the Self-Realization Fellowship in 1920, which now has centers all over the world. Far from drowning in western materialism, he introduced spiritual practices that enabled his students to transform their lives.

to understand Rumi—the Sufi whose spiritual radiance was so great that, apparently, he could even help Jews and Christians to go deeper into their own faiths—we must understand what he called madness. Only then can we hope to get a glimpse of his spiritual rapture, a passion that makes most worldly romances look dull by comparison.

War, greed, hate, violence—none of these things are sane, and yet sadly they form part of the fabric of what we term modern civilization. In fact, even the best of us, if we're not careful, can at times find ourselves so conditioned that we fail to recognize truth when we see it. Meaningless comments such as "that can't be true—it's ridiculous" are among the forms of conditioning that can prevent us from recognizing it.

Truth is not altered one little bit by whether or not we find it ridiculous. It simply *is*.

Persian illumination showing dervishes praying, 1566.

The Japanese spiritual teacher and author Dr Hiroshi Motoyama observed that psychosis and genius are both states of mind that differ from the norm but in different directions. The former is a state further removed from reality than normal, the latter a state closer to reality than normal. The inspired mind of the genius and the demented thought patterns of the psychotic are sometimes lumped together simply on the grounds that neither fits with conventional thinking. Strangely, even when the art of a genius is recognized as being of exceptional quality, still some would put it down to mental illness. Not long ago I read an article by an academic who, while recognizing William Blake's prodigious talent, claimed that he was schizophrenic, in a feeble attempt to explain away Blake's elevated psychic visions as delusion. This is a classic example of an unusual degree of sanity being mistaken for the reverse.

Rumi played on the concept of madness for a higher purpose and this has become a hallmark of his remarkable life and legacy. He described his great spiritual love—which he demonstrated so ardently for his teacher, Shams, and then for the eternal teacher within—as a kind of madness. Thus he highlighted the intensity of his passion, clearly delineating it from conventional notions of spirituality. In actual fact, he was using the term "madness" to describe a higher form of sanity—being, as I believe it was, a degree of enlightenment, albeit one that had not been fully controlled. In some ways, it is unfortunate that Rumi used the concept of madness, because it could exacerbate the views of some that all religion is crazy. But he clearly needed to break free from the restraints imposed by contemporary ideas of what it meant to be spiritual.

RIGHT: *Sufis dancing in a trance, from a Persian watercolor, 1650–55.*

Born in what is now northern Afghanistan in 1207, if mythology is to be believed, young Rumi, the son of a prestigious spiritual teacher, showed signs of his unusual destiny at an early age. Apparently, aged five, he saw visions of the Virgin Mary and the Angel Gabriel, which would have caused consternation among those around him. Another story relates that shortly after one episode, while playing with some other children on the rooftop of his family's home, he literally disappeared. Upon reappearing, he claimed to have been taken into the heavens by men in green cloaks. Whether true or not, the survival of such tales illustrates the longevity of his otherworldly reputation.

When Rumi was about eleven, his family embarked on a migration, moving from place to place until, a decade later, they settled in Konya, Anatolia, which is in present-day Turkey. Years later, in the streets of this thriving city, our second hero of prayer was to meet *his* hero, and the love of his life, Shams al-Din—which literally means "Sun of Religion"—an elderly, wandering mystic.

Rumi, thirty-seven years old and a respected spiritual teacher, lost interest in his family and students, becoming absorbed in adoration of his new guru. Predictably enough, this caused outrage among those who felt he was neglecting them, and the controversy climaxed in Shams al-Din being driven out of Konya less than two years after his arrival. Rumi was distraught.

After a frantic search, Shams was brought back to Konya the following year. Those who had been so hostile to his presence were now resigned to the fact that Rumi's heart would always belong to Shams, regardless of whether they were physically together, although this acquiescence was short-lived. Historical research shows that less than a year later, Shams was murdered.

There is a story that, while grieving for Shams, Rumi swirled round and round a garden pillar and this is what lead to the practice of "whirling", as demonstrated by certain "dervishes", or Muslim ascetics, who spin in an attempt to get closer to God. The idea is that everything, from a tiny atom to a planet, constantly rotates upon a single axis. I also believe that there could be a mystical purpose behind this practice.

But Rumi did not spin in grief forever. The disappearance of his beloved illuminator ultimately led Rumi to seek illumination from within. In the thousands of verses and aphorisms that he composed, we see a reflection of the various stages of his relationship with his guru—love, separation, reunion, and loss—culminating in finding the essence of his beloved within himself.

Whether his words address the heart, the soul, beauty, love, "friend", or anything else, many of them read as impassioned communions with the Divine Source with which he was so desperate for union—and much of his work could be regarded as an unusual but very beautiful form of prayer. Even in translation, the life of every line seems to dance on the page. The themes of madness, drunkenness, and love are weaved in and out of his work in such a way as almost to deceive readers into thinking they are reading the lines of an ordinary romantic love poem, or even a drinking song. But with a heart open to the light imbued in every word, these themes carry with them a mysterious depth underlying the distant attainment of detachment from worldliness and absorption in divinity.

OPPOSITE/ABOVE: *Illustrations from a Madhu-Malati series, showing sufis, c.1799.*

"o my God
don't leave me to the hand of this slippery
     self
don't let me kneel down before anyone
     but you
I run to you from all the tricks and troubles
of 'myself'
I'm yours
don't send me back to myself"

The word "self" here clearly refers to the lower self, which deludes us into believing we are separated from the Divine Source. Once the lower self is conquered, it is possible to be at peace with the higher self, the real self.

"love entered me
and became blood in my veins
emptied me of myself
and filled me with the beloved
every single particle of my body
is soaked in the beloved
my name is all that's left of me
he became the rest"

"what use is there for advice
now that I've fallen into your love?
'tie his feet down' they say about me
but it's my heart that's gone crazy
what's the use of tying my feet?"

"this solitude is better
than being together with thousands
this freedom is sweeter
than owning the whole world
this talking with God
even if only for a very short moment
is better than anything"

"o love
who are you?
you are everything
everything is you ...
... all gold comes from your mind
you are the mother
all of humanity are your children"

abridged from The Rubais of Rumi

OPPOSITE: Detail of "St Teresa of Avila" by Juan de la Miseria, 1570.

all too often it is tempting to regard the life of a
saint as being utterly removed from our own daily lives. It might almost seem
as if they were a different species – born with different DNA, specially pre-
selected by God before birth.

While it is true that we all have a certain destiny, and that this destiny is to
some degree mapped out before birth, it is important for us to remember
that saints are just people. They have to work for their attainment, whether in
this life or – more likely than not – both in this life and in previous lives.
They are not born with angels' wings or haloes. Any special miraculous
power they may have or experience is not by chance. It is not merely a case of

luck. The sanctity that sets them apart
has been earned through loyalty to a
spiritual path, and through making the
sacrifices and following the disciplines
required by that path. It is also very
often the result of true, selfless service
to others and heartfelt love for the
Divine Source.

Very often they are guided by their
higher selves to forsake many of the
conventions to which they have been
conditioned to conform, and to go their

own way—or God's way—rather than the way of orthodoxy. In short, they have a tough time because they do what they believe is right. And providing they are giving service to others, this, in my view, is an extremely admirable way to live.

One of the things that I find so inspiring about St Teresa is that she really struggled on the spiritual path—and won. Through all her trials, both internal and external, she persevered, with results that are miraculous by anybody's standards.

The notoriously tempestuous sculptor Giovanni Lorenzo Bernini (1598–1680) must surely have felt a strange affinity with this larger-than-life character when immortalizing her in marble several decades after her death. Although his passions were worldly and his guiding light physical beauty, while hers were heavenly and the beauty of the soul, by virtue of the very intensity of their respective passions, they shared a common bond. Other people found, and continue to find, this hard to grasp. In my view, it is only when we begin to understand what they went through, rather than just what they achieved, that such passion becomes comprehensible.

St Teresa was born in 1515 in Ávila, Spain. At the tender age of six, she persuaded her older brother Rodrigo to accompany her on a journey to the land of the Moors—a people much feared at the time—with the idea that were they to be killed, they would enter the Kingdom of Heaven quickly. Happily, they were apprehended by a relative long before such a fate could befall them.

During the many years it took Teresa to evolve into the mysterious figure who would become so celebrated for her sanctitude, she tore herself away from the worldliness and vanity she found so tempting, and battled through an almost unbearable resistance to praying. In fact, as a nun, she even considered penances that would have been preferable to what had become for her the nightmare of prayer.

This is very interesting, bearing in mind what was to happen to her later. It would seem that often a particular aversion, or strong negative tendency, if battled and made to surrender, can be transmuted into its exact opposite. Many personal spiritual triumphs are preceded by a feeling of emptiness or internal rebellion, indicating that perhaps such unpleasant experiences have to be mastered before the aspirant develops the necessary maturity to be able to handle the elevated experience that awaits him or her.

Kneeling worshippers, detail from "The Holy Trinity" by Master of Messkirch, (1500–43).

"The Coronation of the Virgin Mary",
Dieric Bouts the Elder, 1455.

During her forties, prayer began to take on a whole new meaning for Teresa, her spiritual labors yielding an unusually rich harvest. Aside from visions of divine beings, we are told that she experienced levitation to such a degree that she had to ask other nuns to hold her habit to try to keep her down. But perhaps the most remarkable of her tales is the one Bernini chose for the subject of his sculpture—the appearance of an angel who seemed to thrust a fire-tipped spear into her heart, causing an intense spiritual and physical pain that sent her into ecstasy. This sensation of love was so wonderful that she prayed for anyone who doubted the truth of her story to be blessed with the same divine experience.

Despite, or more likely because of, these experiences and the trials that preceded them, she didn't lose sight of her mission to spread the love of God to others. She founded numerous convents, often in the face of extreme opposition, and wrote a detailed autobiography, which must have caused quite a stir at the time.

To me, her extraordinary life illustrates the unity of mystical experience, which bridges the divide between religions ordinarily separated by their orthodox dogmas. Had she been born a Hindu, the "miracles" that occurred throughout her life would have been regarded as "siddhis"—the evocation of spiritual powers that can be brought under control by the practice of yoga. Such powers are the result of the rise of the kundalini, although such a concept was unknown to her and pretty well everyone else in sixteenth-century Spain!

to describe Dr George King as a "hero of prayer" seems more than fitting. He took prayer to its highest possible levels, consciously directing love energy in such a way as to bring about results so remarkable they amazed even the most open-minded seeker.

An avid supporter and promoter of spiritual healing, he was especially taken with the idea that this was a skill that could be learned and practiced by virtually anyone. His first experience of giving healing was achieved through the power of prayer, as an eleven-year-old boy.

At that time, 1930, the King family were living in a remote, rural part of the north of England. His mother, Mary King, had been very ill for quite a while. The doctor's frequent visits proved of no avail, so it was suggested that a specialist from the nearest city, which was about twenty miles away, be called to see if he could do any better, but he wasn't able to visit until the following day.

During the night, her young son thought that she was getting worse and, understandably, he wanted to help her. Despite the heavy rain and strong wind, young George King, oil lantern in hand to guide him through the darkness, walked to a clearing in the woods where he used to play. He put the flickering lantern on the rain-soaked ground and stood there, wet and cold, with no idea why he was there or what to do next.

His thoughts wandered to the beauty of the stained-glass window of his local church and he began to pray. The oil lantern went out – his only solace in the face of the stormy blackness gone. Conquering the fear any child would feel in such conditions, he resolved not to let this stop him from saying his prayer. Starting in an orthodox manner, his praying became more intense as he went on, and he felt inspired to raise his hands, palms facing homewards, rather than putting them together in the normal way.

Then, he became aware of a presence. Opening his eyes, he saw a man with long hair and dressed in a flowing robe standing ten to twelve feet away from him, strangely illuminated, although he held no lamp. The man smiled, pointed with his right hand, and said, "Go, your mother is healed," after which he disappeared.

Hastening home, the young boy knew what to expect. His mother was downstairs, being given food – a sight he had not seen in days. Mary King, a clairvoyant and healer, realized what had happened and thanked her son profusely. The following day, she wasted no time in telling the story to the bemused doctor and specialist, who had little choice but to listen to the strange explanation, since they could offer no other in its place.

Many years later, Dr King took up yoga, practising for an average of eight hours a day on top of his full-time job. Following this ancient pathway to illumination helped him to attain staggering heights of consciousness and develop extraordinary psychic abilities.

On one occasion, during the Korean War in the early fifties, he was praying for peace with such power that he levitated off his chair, catching his hair on the ceiling. Like so many men of his generation, he used hair cream and this left a mark on the ceiling. Having a lively sense of humor, he casually told his landlady – a strict Roman Catholic – what had happened, and politely asked her to clean the ceiling and give him the bill. Then off he went, leaving her open-mouthed and no doubt somewhat incredulous.

Detail from mosaic depicting Christ and the Samaritan woman at the well, 6th century.

On returning home from work, he saw that the ceiling had been cleaned, and not long afterwards his landlady came knocking on the door. When he opened it, she stepped back a bit, still shocked by the incident. She was not a little curious, though, saying that she had smelt the mark on the ceiling, compared it with his hair cream and found them to smell the same. Dr King explained again that he had been "just kind of floating round the room".

However, being the spiritual individual that he was, this incident, which he seemed to treat as little more than an interesting experience, proved to serve a greater purpose than just giving his landlady a bit of a shock. She was so affected by it that, a while later, she actually had a vision, which she interpreted as being of the Virgin Mary. The landlady passed on the information imparted by this being to her very unusual tenant, and, we are told, it turned out to be "some of the most marvellous clairvoyance" Dr King had ever been given.

To say that Dr King loved prayer would be an understatement. Never have I come across a man who believed in its power so strongly – a conviction no doubt borne of his understanding of what he knew to be a sacred science. I cannot do justice to how wholeheartedly he promoted it as a tool for personal and global transformation. He was an extremely practical man, and certainly no believer in wishful thinking. The following edited extract from a booklet he published in 1980, entitled *The Truth About Dynamic Prayer*, expresses it much better than anything I could ever write.

*D*ynamic Prayer is a wonderful expression, it is a song of the soul and the soul wants to sing, it wants to express light all around itself, it wants to go forward and help and raise others who need the transmuting power output of a joyous soul. You must allow your inner soul to do this; you must allow this beautiful manifestation to take place, this great surge of energy to fill your mind and aura to such an extent that the bread you cast upon the waters is indeed plentiful and beneficial to all. And the more effort you expend in this respect, the more sure the result must be. This is the Law. If you want an impossible thing it is this: you cannot send out Dynamic Prayers for mankind without having certain results—it is impossible, it cannot be done, the results must come, sooner or later they must come! God, if I could only get this mighty Truth over to the lazy people on this Planet, we would have three and a half billion prayers [the estimated world population at the time] this very morning and before this afternoon, the world would be changed completely!

So, be not deluded by that allegedly logical part of yourself, your conscious mind—but do let your soul sing. It can be taken over by the higher part of you, and the change will be such as to amaze you; and once you have mentally tasted this, you will not want to slip back again. Be all of you thus warned: I have spoken in the light of considerable experience. Heed it, for your sakes, and for the world's.

RIGHT: *Indian miniature of a yogi seated beneath two trees, 1760.*

using the energy of prayer

The number of topics about which we can pray is limitless. There is no problem or situation that cannot benefit from the correct use of prayer, and this section illustrates its versatility. I have selected twenty different headings but there are many more that could be chosen. I suggest you read through all these prayers, and then draw on whatever sections are useful to you at different times in your life.

Alternatively, you may wish to compose your own prayers along the guidelines suggested in Part One. Whichever course you choose, the key thing is not to study prayer—but to practice it.

LEFT: *Detail from "The Last Judgment", by Fra Angelico.*

Action

according to Edmund Burke's aphorism: "All that is necessary for the triumph of evil is that good men do nothing." We have seen this over and over again throughout history. Cruel dictators have become powerful because not enough people did anything to stop them—often because they believed they could do nothing. Injustices have gone unchecked because people didn't want to "rock the boat", or felt it wasn't their place to do anything about it. In short, apathy prevailed.

The good news is that we can all do something that will make a difference to world conditions, and that something is to pray. By sending streams of spiritual energy into the world, the consciousness of the world will change to that degree. As Dr King said, with sufficient spiritual energy all the problems of the world would be solved.

The key fact to remember is that the solution to Earth's multitude of problems is to send out prayer energy to inspire those who can to do the right thing and enable them to continue doing it.

We can also, of course, invoke spiritual energy to inspire ourselves into action, which will help overcome any apathy or lack of motivation we ourselves may feel from time to time.

RIGHT: *Thangka painting depicting the Baishajyaguru, Menla, with seven other Medicine Buddhas, 1780–1880.*

COMMON PRAYER

O Omnipresent Lord! Adorations unto Thee. Give me strength to control the mind and to serve Thee and humanity, untiringly, with great zeal and enthusiasm. Make me a fit instrument for Thy work.

O Loving Presence! Remove my weaknesses, defects and evil thoughts. Make me pure so that I may be able to receive Thy light, grace and blessings.

O Indwelling Presence! Give me a life without disease. Let me remember Thee always. Let me forget the sensual pleasures. Let me have the company of sages and saints. Let me be endowed with dispassion, discrimination and sublime virtues.

O Omniscient Inner Ruler! Prepare me as Thy sweet messenger on this earth so that I may radiate joy, peace and bliss to the whole world. Let this body, mind and senses, be utilized in Thy service and the service of humanity.

O All-merciful Lord! Let me be conscious of my real divine nature. Let me express my divine nature and divine qualities in my daily actions. Let me become a living presence here.

O Omnipotent Power! Breathe unto me Thy breath of Immortality. Let me drink the divine nectar. Lift me up into the highest realm of supreme peace, eternal bliss and divine splendor. Make me dwell in Thee for ever. Salutations unto Thee. O Lord of compassion!

Sri Swami Sivananda (1887–1963), abridged

Travel

from time immemorial, prayers have been said for those who travel. Even the sentiment "have a safe journey" is a kind of blessing—often for the safety of a friend or loved one who is about to travel.

Indian miniature painting of Pilgrims arriving at a shrine to the god Shiva, c. 1760.

Much depends upon the motive behind the journey being undertaken. Obviously a spiritual journey or pilgrimage to a holy place is a far more appropriate journey to pray for than a trip to the supermarket. A journey of rescue, such as an ambulance traveling to an accident or aid-workers being flown to a disaster zone, is undoubtedly even more appropriate.

Mosaic of the harbor in Classe (Portus Classis). Basilica di Sant'Apollinare Nuovo, 6th century.

Nevertheless, all travel can be conducted in the right spiritual manner, and there may be journeys for which you feel inspired to pray.

Here is an interesting example of a Native American travel prayer. While unlikely to be directly applicable to a journey the average modern Westerner is likely to make, it does serve as an example of how we can add description to our prayers, thereby potentially making them more meaningful to us.

ON A VOYAGE

You, O God, are the Lord of the mountains and the valleys. As I travel over mountains and through valleys, I am beneath your feet. You surround me with every kind of creature. Peacocks, pheasants and wild boars cross my path. Open my eyes to see their beauty, that I may perceive them as the work of your hands. In your power, in your thought, all things are abundant.

Sioux prayer

Thankfulness

'*Make your brain live in everlasting thankfulness for experience. Make your heart live in everlasting praise for your Divinity and then—as sure as God—you will be a veritable God.*'

these wonderful words,

channelled by the Master Jesus through Dr King in *The Twelve Blessings*, provide a guideline for life itself.

There is no doubt that gratitude for experiences, whatever they may be, enhances the peaks, and levels out the troughs, of life. A person who is warped by perceptions of injustice, which generally lead to self-pity and frustration, is often miserable. If such people could instead focus on the many things there are to be grateful for, their moods would instantly change, to the benefit of themselves and all of those around them.

There is so much to be thankful for—the majesty of the cosmos, the beauty of the planet upon which we live, the superb works of inspired geniuses throughout history, and so on. It may sound like a platitude, but for those who feel badly treated by life, it would be a useful exercise to sit down and compile a list such as this, and also to look for inspiring stories of those suffering privation or with physical disability who nonetheless manage to remain cheerful by focusing on the positive.

Whether or not thankfulness to God comes naturally to you, it is well worth cultivating, and can lead to a much more fulfilling life in every respect. It is an essential aspect of karma that we express appreciation for what we receive, and feeling thankful in difficult times can be a way through the most testing periods in our lives. Here is a simple Wiccan prayer of thankfulness, which encapsulates some of the things for which we can express gratitude.

A WICCAN PRAYER

Let us give thanks from our hearts
For the blessings of all our good harvest
For the hard-won lessons of life
For the people who bind us together
Making joyful warm hearts out of strife.

And here is an extract from the Jewish scriptures:

EXTRACT FROM PSALM 136

O give thanks unto the LORD, for He is good,
For His mercy endureth forever.
O give thanks unto the God of gods,
For His mercy endureth forever.
O give thanks unto the Lord of lords,
For His mercy endureth forever.

A praying man, Cambodian, 15th/16th century.

"When you arise in the morning, give thanks for the morning light.
Give thanks for your life and your strength.
Give thanks for your food and give thanks for the joy of living.
And if you see no reason for giving thanks, rest assured that the
*   fault is in yourself."*

Chief Tecumseh of the Shawnee Nation (1768–1813)

In more specific terms, the weather is something that people tend to be far quicker to complain about than be thankful for. But, hard though it may be to do so, *whatever* the weather is like, we should *always* try to feel grateful and express this through prayer, be it a silent word or two or an expressive burst of dynamic prayer. We should try to remember that, like every experience, the weather conditions are a result of karma—in this case, our collective karma. Weather is controlled by devas, or nature spirits, who use the energy given to them, consciously or unconsciously, by humankind. Since they work precisely within the confines of karma, these beings have no choice but to use all the energy they are given, good and bad. So, by feeling thankfulness to the devas, and radiating love to nature, you are sending out positive energy, which will actually help to improve weather conditions.

Detail from "Annunciation with
St Joseph and St John the Baptist",
by Filippino Lippi, c.1485.

Angels

'I humbly request that the healing guides may, if they are in a position to do so, assist my dear wife at this time of her need, when I am unable to be with her. Her name is...'

it was a very difficult morning. I was due to run a demonstration of spiritual techniques to an audience of around 500 people at a conference in London. My wife had just dislocated her shoulder and was in agony. While I knew that friends would help to give her healing and take her to hospital if necessary, I still felt awful leaving her—but I also felt duty-bound to attend this demonstration, which involved teaching healing techniques to hundreds of people, and she, being the person that she is, entirely agreed.

Under the circumstances, I decided to request "angelic" help, for want of a better term, as I traveled to the event. I made the plea to my guides, along the lines noted above, clearly stating that this was for my wife, giving her first name and surname.

The reply, which I received through clairaudience (psychic hearing), came in a tone as dry in its humor as it was warm in its compassion: "We do know

RIGHT: *"The Ascension of the Prophet Muhammad",*
probably by Sultan Muhammad, 1539–43.

who your wife is!" Strangely, this response in the form of affectionate banter put me far more at ease than a more formal acknowledgment would have done. It told me that they were probably helping before I even asked them, and my wife did indeed receive considerable healing that day.

This little story illustrates that our spirit guides, or guardian angels, often know a lot more than we may think. They may at times be more aware of the predicaments we face than we are. Nevertheless, we shouldn't underestimate the power of request, since this can serve as a magical trigger, allowing our guides to do more than they would otherwise be permitted to do by karmic law.

I recall one early experience of receiving protection from a guide. Over 25 years ago, I was staying in a hotel in Switzerland while on business for Dr King. Alone in my room at night, I became aware of a dark presence, something I could not only feel but also see, clairvoyantly, although its features remained indistinguishable. Seconds later I became aware of a second presence, that of a huge, powerful-looking Native American spirit guide who slowly, but very

Detail of "The Mystic Nativity", by Sandro Botticelli, 1500.

definitely, commanded the sinister presence to, "Leave this boy *alone!*" And, sure enough, off it went, the Native American guide following it just to make sure that it was gone for good.

While little more than an anecdote, this story is an example of feeling the presence of a guide in a time of need—an experience that is not always limited to those who regard themselves as psychics.

As someone who has had a lot of contact with guides, whom some may term "angels", from the higher realms, as recounted in *Gods, Guides and Guardian Angels*—a book that explains many of the mysteries of this kind of contact—my advice is to be careful when requesting the help of higher beings. Unless you are a proficient psychic and can *safely* channel from the "other side", it is much better to make your requests for this kind of help quite impersonal. Rather than trying to invoke a specific entity or group of entities, just ask for the help of your spirit guides, or angels if you prefer to call them that, in a more general sense. The best way to do this is through prayer.

I must stress that it is not in any way necessary to call on the help of guides or guardian angels. You can go about healing and any other spiritual activity successfully without at any time seeking the help of guides or being aware of their presence. By praying to God, or the Divine Source by any other name, you will invoke whatever help your karma allows you to receive.

But whether you are aware of guides or not, they do exist and they will help you in whatever way they can. The decision about just what they can do is entirely up to them.

There may come a time when you feel the need to request your spirit guides' direct assistance, perhaps with a specific situation, as I did in respect of my wife's shoulder injury. It may be for healing, guidance, or general protection.

Such a prayer should be worded so that it is a request for help, not for something that creates dependence on your guides. It is vital that we stand on our own two feet and don't try to pass the buck for our own lives to any other source, physical or spiritual, and so we should never take this assistance for granted or assume that because we want something we are going to be given it. We should be grateful to our guides merely for giving their consideration to such a request since they have many other things to do, some of them probably far more important than our concerns.

Here is a Native American prayer addressing the "Great Spirit of Our Ancestors". Mention of the pipe should be taken in the context of this tradition, and not as an endorsement of smoking while praying!

ANCESTORS

Oh Great Spirit of our Ancestors,
I raise my pipe to you,
to your messengers the four winds, and to
Mother Earth who provides for your children.
Give us the wisdom to teach our children to
love, to respect and to be kind to each other
so that they may grow with peace in mind.
Let us learn to share all the good things
that you provide for us on this Earth.

LEFT: *"The Angel of the Divine Presence"*,
by William Blake.

Wisdom

the vast difference between knowledge and wisdom is illustrated by the fact that experts in various fields with access to exactly the same information often come to starkly different conclusions. Economists who hold opposite views about the state of the world's finances, medical authorities who prescribe different treatments for the same conditions, and academics who disagree on a whole host of topics all demonstrate that knowledge does not necessarily produce wisdom.

For a wise person, even more important than knowledge is their capacity for love and the ability to express it in practical action. Their intuition, the still small voice within, unfailingly guides them in the right direction. Their wisdom is borne of a balanced fusion between thought and feeling, producing a complete understanding of whatever it is they are focusing upon.

One thing a wise person knows is that they need more wisdom. In fact, the person who doesn't know this, needs it all the more.

LIGHTEN OUR DARKNESS

O eternal light, shine into our hearts;
Eternal goodness, deliver us from despair;
Eternal power, be you our support;
Eternal wisdom, scatter our ignorance.

After Alcuin (735–804)

RIGHT: *Indian miniature depicting an angel and a saint, 1820.*

Clarity

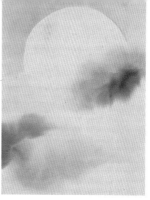

tennyson described a state that had come over him periodically from childhood: "...out of the intensity of consciousness of individuality, the individuality itself seemed to fade away into boundless being, and this not a confused state, but the clearest of the clearest, the surest of the surest, utterly beyond words, where death was almost a laughable impossibility, the loss of personality (if so it were) seeming no extinction but the only true life..." This "clearest of the clearest" state is close to some of the mystical conditions described in eastern writings in which the lower ego is dissolved and unity with the whole is experienced.

Clarity may be the product of logical thinking but it is more the result of intense concentration with a specific focus. Put bluntly, effort produces clarity and laziness causes confusion.

In his timeless aphorisms, Sri Patanjali defines the different mental states we can enter, each one producing more, or less, clarity. Two to avoid are delusion caused by false beliefs, and the use of words that do not relate to their meanings. The first of these is fairly easy to identify while the second is subtler and yet very frequent. In fact, the more one practices exercises in concentration and contemplation, the more aware of it one becomes. How often do people, in the heat of emotion, say things they do not really mean? Prejudice, bias, emotional involvement, and political conviction can cause people to state things as facts when, under close scrutiny, they turn out to be nothing of the sort.

Swami Vivekananda—who in the late nineteenth century was the first great yogi to come to the west, bringing with him the wisdom of the east—was rightly celebrated for his sharp, analytical mind, and deep compassion for humanity. His name means, literally, "bliss (ananda) through discrimination (viveka)".

With total clarity, our lives would take on a whole new dimension. It is an underestimated virtue—and blessing. Confusion is darkness; clarity is light. Every day we are faced with decisions—sometimes big ones, sometimes small ones—but they could all benefit from clarity. These choices make our lives what they are, and clarity makes our lives so much better.

Spiritual illumination is clarity at its height, as illustrated by Tennyson's description. All too often spirituality is treated as something vague, nebulous and unreal, when in fact it is reality in its true sense.

PRAYER FOR CLARITY

Speak, Lord, for thy servant heareth. Grant us ears to hear, eyes to see, wills to obey, hearts to love; then declare what thou wilt, reveal what thou wilt, command what thou wilt, demand what thou wilt—Amen.

Christina Rossetti (1830–94)

PURE AND CLEAR

Make Thou my spirit pure and clear
As are the frosty skies,
Or this first snowdrop of the year
That in my bosom lies.

John Keats (1795–1821)

Bravery

think what could be achieved if we were brave enough. Dare to imagine a life entirely without fear—not without good sense and caution, where necessary, just without the negative energy of fear.

Fear is entirely unnecessary, and extremely counterproductive to fulfilling our life's purpose. Some of our fears we are aware of, and many we are not. Fear of failure and loneliness, insecurities of every kind, fear of thinking beyond our conditioned background—all of these can be conquered through bravery. This liberation from fear leads to fast, effective, lasting spiritual growth, for the greatest application of bravery is to look within. It lies in

probing the recesses of our psyches, no matter what we find, and then illuminating our whole being with the light of understanding and compassion so that we can radiate this light to others. We all feel fear at times, whether it is over something small or something bigger; and very often we are so used to some fears that we don't see them for what they are or realize how much they are holding us back. Through prayer it is possible to expel fear and begin to live the life we were meant to live.

From that which we fear, O Lord, make us fearless.
O bounteous One, assist us with your aid.
Drive far the malevolent, the foeman.

May the atmosphere we breathe
breathe fearlessness into us:
fearlessness on earth
and fearlessness in heaven!
May fearlessness guard us
behind and before!
May fearlessness surround us
above and below!

May we be without fear
of friend and foe!
May we be without fear
of the known and the unknown!
May we be without fear
by night and by day!
Let all the world be my friend!

From The Vedic Experience,
Raimundo Panikkar

OPPOSITE: *Detail from "The Baptism of Christ", by Piero della Francesca, 1450.*

ABOVE: *Wall painting of Vedic god of the elements, 7th/8th century.*

The following is not exactly a prayer, but because of its spiritual content will serve as a very effective tool in transmuting fear when recited with conviction and feeling.

AFFIRMATION OF THE DISCIPLE

I am a point of light within a
   greater Light.
I am a strand of loving energy
   within the stream of Love
   divine.
I am a point of sacrificial Fire,
   focused within the fiery Will
   of God.

And thus I stand

I am a way by which men may
   achieve.
I am a source of strength,
   enabling them to stand.
I am a beam of light, shining
   upon their way.

And thus I stand.

And standing thus, revolve
And tread this way the ways of
   men,
And know the ways of God.

And thus I stand.

Originally published in Telepathy
and the Etheric Vehicle
by Alice Bailey (1880–1949)

This next prayer is very unusual in that it is not asking for yourself, or even for "ourselves", to be brave, but it is asking for *someone else* to be brave.

A WICCAN BLESSING

May the Sun God high in the air
Give you the strength to dare
May the oceans of your soul
Be healed and make you whole.

Guidance

to seek guidance is one thing—who among us hasn't at some time gazed upwards in desperation, thinking "Oh Lord, what should I do?" This is instinctive. But to be genuinely open to receive guidance is something else entirely.

When we ask God what we should do, what are we really saying—not through our words, but from our hearts? Are we really saying: "God, I present myself to you unconditionally, in the hope that I may receive your guidance, whatever it may be, and that I will then follow it completely?" Or are we saying: "God, please get me out of this mess I'm in at the moment, solve my problems for me, with minimal effort on my part, so I can just carry on doing what I want to do, without this current problem getting in the way?" The difference between these two approaches could be the difference between success and failure in receiving divine guidance.

Actually, the answers to all the questions we could ever pose are to be found within ourselves. It is our own higher self we should be guided by at all times. Very often in difficult situations, it is not the finding of an answer that is the real problem, but having the courage and self-discipline to act upon it. If we stop and think, we generally know what we should do, but when we don't want to do it, the issue becomes complex and confusing. That's when we should remember that the inner voice will never guide us wrongly—all we need is the ability to hear what it is saying and the strength to follow it.

Having written, taught, and broadcast extensively to millions of people about how to unlock their psychic powers, there is one thing of which I am absolutely sure—the greatest of all the powers, which in some ways is above psychic ability, is intuition. It is always right—after all, it is the link with our divine self.

One way the inner voice can speak to us is through our conscience. Think of the conscience as being like a muscle. The more it is used, the stronger it becomes, albeit sometimes causing aches and pains along the way. Guilt can be a dirty word in much of the New Age movement, but the truth is that there's nothing wrong with a bit of guilt, providing it is appropriate. Where guilt goes wrong is when it is either misplaced or becomes an obsession. It is valid as long as it guides us to put right something in our lives—after that, it can become a form of emotional self-indulgence, sometimes bordering on masochism.

We should all try to listen to our intuition and, where appropriate, to our conscience, and follow it. The more we do this, the louder the voice will be, and the clearer our guidance, until we come to know intuitively what is right. It can be difficult, because often what we know to be right compels us into doing something that is a long way from what we would normally want to do. But the strength and clarity that come from making the right decisions bring with them liberation from the confusion and complex excuses offered by our lower selves. Life becomes so much simpler, which is a wonderful feeling.

The following very unusual prayer, by Sir Francis Drake, is a prayer for constant guidance from our higher selves. To me, it encapsulates the toughness of a genuine spiritual approach. This is someone who is not searching so much

LEFT: *Detail from "Tobias and the Archangel Raphael", by Domenico di Michelino, 1480.*

for the easiness of peace as for the struggle of self-improvement, which is the only way to achieve lasting peace. If this prayer is anything to go by, Sir Francis was not just a naval genius but possessed an unusual degree of honesty and self-realization. He was clearly not one to rest on the laurels of his celebrated achievements, or take the easy option, but sought to reach higher levels.

PRAYER OF SIR FRANCIS DRAKE

Disturb us, Lord, when we are
    too well pleased with
    ourselves,
When our dreams have come
    true
Because we have dreamed too
    little,
When we arrived safely
Because we sailed too close to
    the shore.

Disturb us, Lord, when
With the abundance of things
    we possess
We have lost our thirst
For the waters of life;
Having fallen in love with life,
We have ceased to dream of
eternity
And in our efforts to build a
    new earth,
We have allowed our vision
Of the new Heaven to dim.

Disturb us, Lord, to dare
    more boldly,
To venture on wider seas
Where storms will show your
    mastery;
Where losing sight of land,
We shall find the stars.
We ask You to push back
The horizons of our hopes;
And to push into the future
In strength, courage, hope,
    and love.

Sir Francis Drake, 1540–96

Children

childhood is an
immensely important time. A "good" childhood
is no guarantee that a child will turn out well any
more than a "difficult" one inevitably means that
a child will turn out badly. But the responsibility of parents to do everything
they can to guide children towards the light, steering them away from the
dark confusion that could otherwise permanently cloud their lives, is a heavy
one. It is far from easy. There are times when even those with a degree of
spiritual awareness can be stuck about what advice or guidance to give
children, let alone how to give it.

I do not speak from personal experience in this respect. Alyson and I
chose not to be parents because we wanted to devote ourselves more
completely to a life of spiritual service to the world as a whole. However,
many others are truly inspired by the prospect of giving the right love and
guidance to their children, and often make real sacrifices to do so.

Most parents have the welfare of their children at heart and for them prayer
can be such a help. We can pray for wisdom, so that we can pass it on to
children, we can pray for guidance in how to pass it on, and we can pray that the
light of wisdom imbues children directly. Having less developed conscious
minds than adults, children are often less resistant to the energy invoked
through prayer, and may respond more quickly to it, whether it be a prayer for
their illumination or healing.

✓ May light, which can take hold of you, flow into you.
I accompany its rays with the warmth of my love.
I think with my thinking's best
thoughts of joy
Of your heart's stirrings.
These thoughts are to strengthen
you,
They are to carry you,
They are to give you clarity.
I would like to gather, before the
steps of your life,
My thoughts of joy,
So that they may join forces with
your will for life
And that this will may be strong
In all the world,
Ever more,
By virtue of its own power.

*Rudolf Steiner (1861–1925), developer
of "anthroposophy", whose radical
approach to education is still practised
today in schools bearing his name.*

FOR A NEWBORN

I lift up this newborn child
to you.
You brought it to birth, you
gave it life.
This child is a fresh bud on
an ancient tree,
A new member of an old
family.
May this fresh bud
blossom.
May this child grow strong
and righteous.

Kalahari bushmen's song, Africa

RIGHT: *"Adoration of
the Shepherds", by Lorenzo
di Credi, c.1510.*

Compassion

we all feel compassion, in different ways, at different times, and we can all manifest it through prayer as well as in a host of other ways. And manifesting it is vital— compassion is of little use to those for whom we feel it unless we try to put it into practical action.

Compassion means feeling other people's suffering as if it were your own. When we pray, this feeling becomes the love in which the energy of the prayer is carried to its destination. It is the most natural feeling in the world and, while it should be controlled, it should never be restricted, or ignored. Compassion is generated by the divine essence within us, that is to say our spirit, the essence of all things, and when its power is manifested through our souls it prompts feeling for all, inspiring us to pray. Remember Dr King's beautiful description of dynamic prayer: "It is the song of the soul and the soul wants to sing."

We should not mistake compassion for sentimentality. They may both taste sweet but one is pure, natural, healthy honey, and the other is sickly, over-refined, white sugar. Compassion is an urge springing from our innate knowledge of the oneness of everything in creation. Sentimentality, on the other hand, is tangled in the undergrowth of materialism and is to be avoided on the spiritual path, even though at first glance it may sometimes *seem* similar to, and even synonymous with, compassion.

Sometimes we may be so overwhelmed with compassion that we just have to act. This intensity of feeling, when controlled and taken on to a higher level, gives a fantastic impetus to our prayers. Although, when praying for people we have never met who are suffering in distant corners of the globe, we may never consciously know what difference our prayers have made, our higher selves *will* know. We will also be released from a prison of psychic and spiritual frustration by acting in this way, which can lead to a deep feeling of inner peace.

A Prayer for Humility and Charity to Grow Within Us

Incline us O God to think humbly of ourselves, to be saved only in the examination of our own conduct, to consider our fellow-creatures with kindness, and to judge of all they say and do with the charity which we would desire from them ourselves.

Jane Austen (1775–1817)

Detail from "The Meeting of St Dominic and St Francis", a 15th century painting of the Italian School.

A MUSLIM PRAYER ABOUT LOVE

God made this universe from love
For Him to be the Father of.
There cannot be another such as He.

What duty more exquisite is
Than loving with a love like His?
A better task
No one could ever ask.

Rahman Baba (16th/17th century)

A THEOSOPHICAL PRAYER ABOUT ONENESS

O Hidden Life, vibrant in every atom,
O Hidden Light, shining in every creature,
O Hidden Love, embracing all in Oneness,
May each who feels himself as one with Thee
Know he is therefore one with every other.

Annie Besant (1847–1933)

RIGHT: *"Sultan Mahmud I of Turkey",
holding prayer beads, 18th century.*

Healing

this is so natural that at times it seems hard *not* to give it. If any subject deserves to be featured twice in a book on prayer (as it is in this one), it's certainly healing!

I believe that certain doctors and nurses, for example, even if they don't know anything about spiritual healing, simply by virtue of their desire to help someone in need, will automatically radiate love through themselves to the person they are treating. A similar example is a parent's instinctive tendency to "rub it better" when a child hurts him or herself. The physical contact is a way of transmitting spiritual energy directly from the parent to the area of discomfort in the child. Likewise, holding someone's hand, or giving them a hug when they are upset can have a healing effect.

I would recommend everyone to learn a *bona fide* form of spiritual healing, and to choose a simple one to start with that can be learned in a day and practiced for life. There are many effective schools of hands-on healing, including several from the reiki tradition. Most involve placing your hands over the major chakras. This contact healing is in many ways similar to prayer, in that it involves invoking energy, conditioning it with love, and directing it to where it is needed. Often we are in a situation where distance, time, and other factors prevent us from performing contact healing, but we can all say a healing prayer.

LEFT: *Detail from an Indian miniature depicting a yogi practicing asanas, 1760.*

A Healing Prayer

Oh Divine Spirit behind all life,
I request that I may be a channel
for your healing power
To flow to [INSERT THE NAME/S OF THE
PERSON/PEOPLE YOU WISH TO HEAL]
I request that he/she/they may be
strengthened at this time
With your great love and
revitalizing energy
At every level of their being.
I give thanks for the opportunity of
being used
As a channel for your healing
power at this time.
May Thy Divine will be done.

*Detail from "The Meeting of King
Solomon and the Queen of
Sheba", from the original panel
from the East Doors of the
Baptistery by Lorenzo Ghiberti,
1425–52.*

Please note that while saying this prayer you should visualize the recipient
or recipients in robust good health and surrounded by white light,
regardless of whatever condition you know them to be in. Depending on
how much time you have available, leave a considerable gap between each
name if you are sending healing to more than one person, allowing the
power to flow through you to them individually as you do so.

Animals

some sections of this book require more explanation than others—this one needs very little. Animal lovers know that their pets respond to energy and react quickly to moods and atmospheres; there are numerous examples of their psychic attributes.

Animals respond to healing just as much as human beings—in fact, often even more so, since they tend to have less resistance to the flow of energy. The healing prayer (opposite) was written with human beings in mind, but could work just as well for an animal that is suffering. If you don't know the creature's name, describe the animal you mean, giving its location or some other distinguishing details.

The love we feel for animals should not be limited to our own pets, however, but should be extended to the whole animal kingdom, much of which is in terrible pain as a result of human beings and their activities. Significantly, the Great Prayer Festival of Tibet (Monlam Chenmo), which was founded in 1409 and is held annually, includes prayers for the good of all beings—animal as well as human. We all have a responsibility to the animal kingdom and it can become an important part of our prayer life.

The following prayer not only sends love to the entire animal kingdom, but seeks to inspire those who would maltreat animals to rise above their foul limitation to gain an appreciation of the sanctity of all life.

Oh Divine and Wondrous Creator,
Thou which art behind all things,
I ask to be used as a channel
For Thy Divine Power
To flow in a stream of radiant Light
To the animal kingdom
Which has been so greatly abused by man.

My heart is filled with love for God's creatures
Who are part of the abundance of manifestation,
Part of the Oneness of all Life.
May these ones be filled
With Thy warmth and Thy Love
So that they may live their lives
Free from any suffering inflicted upon them
By the cruelty of human beings.

May Thy power, love and inspiration
Flow unto those who would cause suffering
To the animal kingdom,
That they may rise above
Their self-imposed limitation
And be inspired by the realization that all life is sacred
In its many and myriad forms.

Let us always be guided by
The Divine Spark within
So that the seeds of unselfishness
May grow and blossom into flowers of eternal wisdom
And open up our hearts to eternal Truth.   *Alyson Lawrence*

*Detail of "The Good Shepherd" from a mosaic in the mausoleum of Empress
Galla Placidia. Ravenna, Italy, c.440.*

Much though we may like animals, it is important to note that some can be dangerous. Naturally, all sensible precautions should be taken when dealing with such creatures but, even without touching them, prayer can sometimes be surprisingly effective. A friend of mine recently recounted a story about a large swarm of bees that had moved into her front garden. Her friends and neighbors expressed considerable alarm and were unanimous in urging her to have them removed—which would have been expensive, and, more seriously as far as my friend was concerned, very bad news for the bees.

She decided to say a few words of prayer, anxious that the bees would not be harmed in any way. Standing in the safety of her living room, she looked out of the window at the bees and spoke to them mentally, explaining that she was about to say a prayer to help them to find somewhere safe to live. Then she began to send them her love in a powerful way, something she is very good at, having been practising dynamic prayer for many years.

A few minutes later she heard a loud rush of buzzing, and watched—amazed—as the entire swarm flew over her house and off in the direction of some nearby woodland.

Detail of animals from an engraved piece of walrus ivory, Inuit people.

Destiny

your destiny is written, but you are the editor. More precisely, our higher selves write our destinies and our conscious selves are given the task of accessing this knowledge and putting it into practice. This is something we can all do. Karma never presents anyone with a task that is beyond them.

Learning about, and living up to, our destiny is perhaps the single most important task that any of us have to underake, because all other tasks— and opportunities for growth—spring from it.

Some people may not think about, or even believe in, destiny, and yet still they manage to adhere to it, simply by following the guidance of their higher selves at key moments in their lives, whether conciously or unconciously.

Detail of a statue of Brahma in heroic posture.

These people may have no idea at all why they are making the choices they are making, while others have a very strong sense of destiny, and consciously set out to fulfill it—Sir Winston Churchill and Richard Wagner are obvious examples. This clear sense of purpose, and even of imminent greatness, can make a person seem arrogant, but recognition of truth should never be mistaken for arrogance. On the contrary, it is the hallmark of humility, because it is recognition of the greatness of the Divine.

To reflect that each and every one of us, however apparently insignificant, has a destiny written by the highest, most divine part of ourselves is extremely inspiring. What's more, this destiny is always positive. No one is destined to be bad. Even the worst dictators, while their experience pattern may have cultivated negative traits for lives and lives, still have the chance, however improbable, of being good. And one day, no matter how long it takes, we will all achieve our ultimate destiny—union with the Divine Source.

Not all destinies are glamorous. Destiny does not imply fame or even necessarily great skill. Destiny is just what you are meant to do—it doesn't involve trying to do what someone else is meant to do. But we should never regard destiny as a limiting factor in our lives—even if our lot is comparatively modest, it is possible to exceed its boundaries and create a new and higher destiny. This may happen rarely, but it is nevertheless important for us all to remember that the higher we gaze, the higher we can fly. As Michelangelo so brilliantly put it: "The greater danger for most of us is not that our aim is too high and we miss it, but that it is too low and we reach it."

RIGHT: *Diana or the Moon from a series of reliefs depicting the planetary symbols and signs of the zodiac, by Agostino di Duccio, c.1450.*

My Soul's Purpose

Oh wondrous Creator of Life,
As the Moon, the Stars and the Sun
Shine in accordance with Your Plan;
As the Galaxy, filled with teeming life,
Evolves in its journey back to You;
I beseech, with humble heart,
That I too may unfold my soul's purpose;
The higher, brighter path that You,
In Your mysterious and infinite wisdom,
Would surely have me tread.

I ask, oh mighty Brahma,
That Your everlasting love transforms
My every word, thought and action;
And that my steps be straight and true
In my sacred journey back to You.
Oh God of the Universe, Author of its Laws,
May I light the way for others
As a loving instrument of Your peace;
May the wonder of my destiny be fulfilled
And Your Divine will be done.

Chrissie Blaze

Devotion

the cornerstone

of spiritual and religious belief and practice, devotion takes many forms but all of them are essentially about the same thing. In the yoga tradition, this is known as "bhakti": union with God through devotion.

The devotion a disciple feels for his teacher, guru, or master is a wonderful, pure love. In a truly spiritual relationship such as this, the strong, impersonal love that results from detachment from worldliness can be applied in a personal way and directed toward a single individual. The love is personal because it is felt by one person for another whom they know and revere above everyone else, but impersonal because it is unselfish and stems from a love of truth—or God as truth—and nothing else.

A student does not—or should not—love his spiritual teacher because he or she is good-looking, has an engaging sense of humor, is an excellent athlete, or has psychic powers, but because the teacher is a living incarnation of a degree of truth higher than that which the student has yet experienced. The student should love his teacher because of his or her wisdom, which is love in practical action. Wisdom is like a lighthouse from which love shines, illuminating the choppy seas of materialism for all the many ships that have lost their way.

The focus of such devotion, and the subject of this spiritually intimate, personal relationship, need not be a teacher you have met—or will ever meet.

Your devotion could, for example, be to an avatar such as Confucius, who lived on the other side of the world two and a half thousand years ago. The choice of the teacher you follow should be determined not by convenience but by the caliber of their teachings and by how useful they are in the world today. We should seek a teacher truly worthy of our devotion. For instance, I believe Confucius taught an outstanding message to the people of China at that time, but to apply the fundamental principles of Confucianism to the modern world in a productive way would be quite a challenge. Another problem is the question of how much of Confucius's real teachings—and those of other great avatars of antiquity—have reached modernity unsullied, in the pure form in which they were given.

Devotion to your teacher—if the teacher is a genuine Master in the highest sense of the word—should be absolute. This doesn't mean that you need reject the teachings of others, or regard all other teachers as wrong. It is simply that your Master should come first in your life—in fact not just first, but second, third, and fourth as well.

Devotion to God does not have to be expressed through a teacher, though. It can be expressed through a love for humanity as a whole, or through working for a particular cause for the improvement of the world. In some ways, this is an even better approach to take. You could be an atheist and express such devotion, which illustrates the potential for unselfishness that can be achieved through bhakti yoga. In secular humanism, there is no question of God doing anything for us, because the notion of God is rejected.

RIGHT: *Stone engraving of Confucius.*

A very potent prayer is one *for*, rather than *to*, a divine being. In other words, instead of praying to Jesus, Buddha, or any other deity to help us, how much better it would be to pray that *we* might be able to help *them*, by sending our love and appreciation to them and by serving their cause?

O LORD! I SURRENDER MYSELF UNTO THEE

O Lord! I surrender myself unto Thee.
Here is my body; take it.
Utilize it in any way Thou likest.
Here is my mind; take it.
Here is my soul, my will, my heart,
My energy, my strength, my wealth,
My property—all that I have.
I am Thine; all is Thine, my Lord.
Thy will be done.

Sri Swami Sivananda (1887–1963),
abridged

RIGHT: *Detail from "The Ascension of Christ", by Giotto, 1303.*

Our maintenance is in nobody's power but God's:
To all of us but one hope abideth
There is one: is there any other?
There is only Thou, there is only Thou, O God!

Birds have no money in their possession
They only depend on trees and water.
God is their Giver.
There is only Thou, there is only Thou, O God!

From The Sikh Religion, Volume 1, *by Max Arthur MacAuliffe*

Psalm 117

O praise the LORD, all ye nations;
Laud Him, all ye peoples.
For His mercy is great toward us;
And the truth of the LORD endureth for ever.
Hallelujah.

From the Jewish scriptures

Blessing

just like prayer, blessing is a way of sending love to a focal point. Also just like prayer, it can be used in several ways—to protect, heal, uplift, guide, thank, and, on occasion, help extinguish the fire of hate in the hearts of others, and even in our own hearts, if necessary. Sometimes blessing is performed through ordinary prayer, and sometimes in other ways, such as through a specific hand sign, or mudra.

The New Age series of *Twelve Blessings* given to Dr King is as follows:

Blessed are they who work for peace
Blessed are the wise ones
Blessed are they who love
Blessed are the Planetary Ones
Blessed are the Thanksgivers
Blessed are they who heal
Blessed is the Mother Earth
Blessed is the mighty Sun
Blessed are the Supreme Lords of Karma
Blessed is the great being known as the Galaxy
Blessed are the Supreme Lords of Creation
Blessed is the Absolute

Each blessing reveals the spiritual significance of its subject and helps us to gain a better appreciation of our place in the world and the cosmos. The performance of a blessing incorporates the visualization technique described on page 26. Many of the blessings are followed by beautiful prayers for the uplifting of humanity. I regard these as the finest prayers I know and use them regularly. Here is an example:

WE GLORIFY THEE

Oh Divine Lord of all Wondrous Creation,
We raise our voices and minds to You—NOW—in prayer.
Knowing even as we do, that this is answered at this moment.
Oh Wondrous God,
We ask that the hearts and minds of man
Might be opened to Thy Presence,
To Thy Mighty Light.
So that they may forever Glorify Thee.
So that they may realize that within them
Beats a Spark directly connected to
Thy Wondrous Heart.
We raise our minds in thankfulness
For the fulfillment of our prayer.
For this SHALL come to pass
Upon this Earth.

Some of these blessings and prayers are used in a mission devised by Dr King, which has been featured extensively in the media. It is known as "Operation Prayer Power"and combines the practice of *The Twelve Blessings* with the chanting of certain holy mantras. The energy invoked is stored in a physical container, called an Operation Prayer Power battery. Drawing on the science of radionics, and using the capacity of crystals to contain psychic energies, hundreds of

Detail of the hand of Jesus, from a mosaic in Sant'Apollinare Nuovo, Ravenna, Italy, 6th century.

hours of stored prayer energy are thus saved to be released in a matter of minutes during significant world crises, such as war, famine, and earthquakes.

The results of such releases have been carefully monitored for over thirty years. Some of them have been startling in their impact and in the positive changes they have wrought. Dr King's mission is currently performed in five locations—London and Barnsley in the UK, Los Angeles and Michigan in the USA, and Auckland in New Zealand. It is well worth investigating and, if you are able, supporting.

LEFT: *Fragment from a wall painting depicting a Buddhist paradise, from Duldur-Aqur, Xinjiang, c.700.*

Blessings can be performed in many situations in life. With the right feeling and an appropriately worded prayer, even if it is just a few words long, all of life—human, animal, and plant—can be blessed, as can inanimate objects, such as buildings, vehicles, and food. For those who like to say grace before eating, I must offer a word of advice—if you specifically bless your food, try to eat every morsel of it. Of course, you can say grace without blessing the food, but if you do bless it, make sure that it is something you intend to eat!

GRACE

Oh Mighty God,
We give thanks for the food
and drink upon our table,
To provide sustenance for our
journey back to you.
May we use this energy you
have given to us
By living our lives as you would
have us do.
Thy will be done this day.

From "The Marriage at Cana"; the blessing of water into wine.

The act of blessing creates an energy that will start to fill your whole life with a spiritual quality and a deep inner feeling of satisfaction. It comes from the soul and is one sure way to connect with the higher part of our being.

Cosmos

when we contemplate the vastness of the cosmos, how can we fail to be anything but awed by its magnitude, its diversity, and the sheer power of the wonderment it engenders. That we are part of something so utterly amazing beggars belief, but part of it we are.

The more we reflect upon the incredible nature of the cosmos, the more we are able to appreciate the true nature of ourselves. For not only are we all essential parts of the cosmos, but we *are* the cosmos itself. Without the illusion of space and time, all that ever was and is and will be is ONE—a single, supreme flame burning in the potential of non-existence, illuminating the great void, lighting the very essence of light itself. Life is but a single organism and the force behind life but a single divine power. And, according to ancient Hindu writings, this power is the essence of who and what we all are. All we need to do is to realize it.

As if thoughts such as these were not enough, it serves us well also to reflect that the great bodies within creation are not just the lifeless products of millennia of chemical reactions—they themselves are living entities. The Earth, the Sun, and even the galaxy that provides us with a home are all alive, and one day in the seemingly impossibly distant dawn of illumination, we will become one with great beings such as these, an amalgam of souls united in perfect love. When the lessons of this Earth have been learned, we will move onward in an ever-more exhilarating journey back to the Godhead. We will experience the myriad beauties of manifestation envisioned by the divine architect before eternity began and the roaring wave of infinity broke upon the shore of total silence.

With these inspiring thoughts in mind, the following beautiful prayer from *The Twelve Blessings* is the perfect one to say.

PRAYER FOR THE GALAXY

Oh Divine One, Who allows us within Thy Body,
Take from our hearts our Love
Into Thine Own Self—this very moment.
We make this sacrifice for we dimly realize
Thy Greatness.
Oh Mighty Jehovah, Lord of Creation,
Compassionate Master of all Life,
Controller of Manifestation,
To Thee we offer our prayer of
Everlasting thankfulness, for the sacrifice
Continually made by Thy Wondrous Angel.
Preserve this One for Its allotted time.
Then, Oh Jehovah, Lord of Lords,
Transmute it into the
Center of Centers within Thy Mind.

RIGHT: *"God the Father", from the Psalter of Pope Paul III, by Vincenzio Raimondo, 1542.*

Channelled through Dr George King by The Master Jesus

Earth

the quantum leap that humanity has made in recent years in terms of ecological awareness is a fantastic step forward. It shows a recognition of the consequences of our actions, which is essential to our survival as a race. It also forces us to take a much more global outlook. The pollution produced by one country not only causes the people of that country to suffer but affects other countries as well.

However, this human-orientated view of ecology is still a long way from a spiritual appreciation of the true nature of the Earth herself. It's great to look after the environment for the sake of humanity, but it's even better to do it *for the sake of the Earth*. The so-called primitive traditions of the Native Americans, Australian Aborigines, and others in revering the Earth, are in fact, from a spiritual point of view, much more advanced than the so-called "sophistication" of the atom bomb or any of the other destructive chimeras of modern science.

Let us, as we sit in our offices, wearing comfortable clothes, gazing at computer screens, allow our consciences to drift back to that state of innocent, instinctive awareness that, without her—Gaia, as she was known in ancient Greece, the Mother of us all—we would be homeless. We should give thanks every day for the ground beneath our feet. Contemplate, with all your heart and soul, the concept that a great goddess veils herself in a material

LEFT: *"Allegory of Earth", by Cornelis and Paul de Vos, 17th century, depicting the overflowing cornucopia and bounty of Mother Earth.*

form, so that we, infinitesimally small and insignificant by comparison, may live, love, serve, and grow as we ought to do. Think of her sacrifice and allow yourself to be awed by it. Consider the analogy of a great enlightened sage, who is capable of entering a state of supreme bliss, who instead dresses in rags so that ants may crawl across her body, biting, gnawing, and scuttling about with scarcely the most fleeting of thoughts for the sacred flesh beneath their feet.

Thoughts like these—radical and even disturbing—are the thoughts from which a true appreciation of Mother Earth will grow, blossom, and bear the fruit of wisdom. The following simple prayer can be a vehicle for expressing this sort of devotion.

A PRAYER FOR THE MOTHER EARTH

Oh Divine Source of all life,
May your love go out to the Mother Earth,
For Her great sacrifice;
May your light go out to the Mother Earth,
For her profound compassion.
May She be blessed now and always.

While the Earth as goddess should be the main focus of prayers about the planet, there is nothing wrong with showing our appreciation of the fruits of the land as well, providing this is secondary to our love for the Earth as a spiritual entity. The following few lines express very eloquently the thoughts of a great English herbalist on this subject.

What greater delight is there than to behold the earth apparelled with plants as with a robe of embroidered works, set with Orient pearls and garnished with the great diversity of rare and costly jewels. But these delights are in the outward senses. The principal delight is in the mind, singularly enriched with the knowledge of these visible things, setting forth to us the invisible wisdom and admirable workmanship of almighty God.

John Gerard (1545–1612)

Gaia, Mother Earth, AD 275.

Success

surely one of the most misunderstood concepts is success. According to surveys of schoolchildren, many of them regard the greatest possible achievement in this life as becoming famous—not as having exhibited great skill in entertainment, the arts, sport, or any other field of activity, but just fame for its own sake. Clearly the line between famous and infamous has become blurred to the point where even dubious characters, just because they are celebrities, are placed on the same pedestal as those who have really achieved something.

Writer G.K. Chesterton said that he spent the whole of his life discovering the truth contained in platitudes. My definition of success falls into the category of being a platitude but is also true: success is measured by how much you change the world for the better.

Another way of measuring success is by the degree to which you realise your inner potential. Success, after all, is personal attainment. It lies both in achieving your goals of service to others and manifesting the capacity of your inner self.

The greatest and most successful act is undoubtedly one of service to others. This is epitomized by the following French prayer, written in the spirit of St Francis of Assisi, which has been translated by Mark Bennett:

Lord, make me an instrument of your peace.
Where there is hate, may I bring love.
Where there is transgression, forgiveness.
Where there is discord, union.
Where there is error, truth.
Where there is doubt, faith.
Where there is despair, hope.
Where there is darkness, light.
Where there is sadness, joy.
Oh Master, may I seek not so much to be consoled, as to console;
To be understood, as to understand;
To be loved, as to love –
For it is in giving, that one receives;
It is in forgetting oneself, that one finds;
It is in forgiving, that one is forgiven;
It is in transcending death that one rises to eternal life.

RIGHT: *Detail from "Portrait of the Artist's Sister in the Garb of a Nun", by Sofonisba Anguissola, 16th century.*

Peace

according to Taoism, when the mind is still, the whole universe surrenders to it. Our modern world has all but lost sight of the value of inner peace. Instead, the quest seems to be for ever more stimulation and adrenalin-fuelled activity. Material advancement, the demands of family, increasing work pressures, intense leisure pursuits, and unhealthy doses of stimulants all combine to make inner peace a distant dream for many.

The result? Unprecedented stress levels borne out by numerous surveys and medical studies. Work-related organizations report an all-time high of absences or time off taken due to stress-related illness.

Many believe that peace is found through relaxation pursuits. Certainly these can be beneficial, but the deeper states of peace and, indeed, bliss are far too active to be the product of just relaxation. According to the Hindu Upanishads, when we let the urges of our lower will subside like waves into the sea of peace, we contact our real selves. This, they said, can be achieved through meditation and detachment from material pursuits.

In this day and age, an even greater path than this is recommended, namely to focus on the suffering of others rather than ourselves. We cannot be unduly concerned about our own relatively petty problems when we look at the conditions endured in war-torn or disaster regions around the world, where the people are in desperate need of help.

By working for world peace you will discover inner peace, and there is no finer way to do this than by sending out prayer energy. Here is an abridged version of a beautiful prayer written by the great yogi Swami Sivananda, which you can use.

PRAYER FOR WORLD PEACE

O Adorable Lord! May absolute peace reign over the whole world. May the war come to an end soon. May all nations and communities be united by the bond of pure love. May all enjoy peace and prosperity. May there be deep abiding peace throughout the universe. Grant us eternal peace, the peace that passeth all understanding. May we all work together harmoniously with the spirit of self-sacrifice for the well-being of the world. May we all develop cosmic love and universal brotherhood. May we all see God in all faces!

O All-merciful Lord! Grant us an understanding and forgiving heart, broad tolerance and adaptability. O Lord! Grant us the inner eye of wisdom, with which we will behold the Oneness of the Self everywhere.

Peace be to the East. Peace be to the West. Peace be to the North. Peace be to the South. Peace be above. Peace be below. Peace be to all the creatures of this universe.

Sri Swami Sivananda (1887–1963), abridged

Whereas happiness created through stimulation and selfishness always subsides and dies, spiritual happiness resulting from inner peace is lasting. There may be occasions when you will need to leave this inner peace because your conscience will direct you to do so in service to others. But it will always be there and you will be able to return to it whenever the opportunity arises.

I must say that those so-called teachers who claim to be in permanent peace and always happy, for me, fail the spiritual test. I believe that spiritual giants, such as Swami Vivekananda, went through periods of stark despair as well as incredible elation. One could hardly describe the life of the Master Jesus as a happy one; and it was due to compassion and sadness through coming into contact with the true suffering of others that the Lord Buddha decided to devote himself entirely to the spiritual path.

"Happy is the arising of the awakened, happy is the teaching of the True Law, happy is peace in the church, happy is the devotion of those who are at peace."

From The Dhammapada, *verse 194*

Inner peace is there for all of us to find. One thing I can vouch for, even from my limited experience, is that there is an unfathomable peace that is so profound as to be almost disturbing. I had a small glimpse of this a couple of years ago when I experienced a state of such peace that everything was just totally right—that's the only phrase I can use. I described it at the time as follows:

RIGHT: *"Japanese Lady Reading by Moonlight",*
by Keisai Yeisen, 19th century.

Seeping through my sinews
Engulfing the innermost recesses of my being,
Perfect peace—quiescent—satisfied—replete.
How could this be?
"Because it's right" came the answer.
Rightness flowing through my veins—
Now all is possible.
A force beyond reason,
Yet logical to its core.
Who can argue with that?
And who would want to!

A prayerful life can, at the right time and in the right way, undoubtedly be a peaceful life. The following extract from Psalm 23, I believe is a metaphor for the peace that comes from walking the spiritual path.

EXTRACT FROM PSALM 23

The LORD is my shepherd; I shall not want.
He maketh me to lie down in green pastures;
He leadeth me beside the still waters.
He restoreth my soul;
He guideth me in straight paths for His name's sake.

From the Jewish scriptures.

World

the final section of this book is, in my
view, the most important of all. As you will have realized by now, I don't
consider that there is any more significant or potent use of prayer than for
the world as a whole.

There are many prayers you can use in this context, one of the greatest of
which is undoubtedly "The New Lord's Prayer" on page 31. Here is another
prayer you can use for the betterment and well-being of the world.

Detail from a Native American needlework depicting the creation of the
world, 1925.

Oh mighty God—which is the light which shines through
   and behind all things,
We pray that Your wondrous power of love may fall
   upon our troubled world—now!
May it fill the hearts and minds of all those who are
   suffering and in need at this time—
May it manifest as a great healing light, to give comfort
   to those who are sick—
May it uplift those who feel abandoned in their loneliness
   and despair—
May it inspire those who have the responsibility of
   world leadership
To bring lasting peace to our planet.
Oh wondrous God, may we be given the power and strength
To reach forever inwards and upwards towards our Divinity,
So that we may always be mindful of the ONENESS of all life.

Ray Nielsen

It is agreed by the greatest yogis and truest mystics that the most profound
state of meditation anyone can experience is a state of "oneness". In this
state, it is said that you don't just believe in oneness, or even feel a sense of
oneness; you know from personal experience that we are all "one". The only
logical conclusion of such enlightenment as this is to dedicate ourselves in

service to the world as a whole and to all life upon it. Indeed, this is exactly what enlightened men and women have always done.

As John Donne put it, "No man is an island, entire of itself; every man is a piece of the continent, a part of the main." By praying for the world, you are demonstrating that you have grasped this reality and feel a sense of responsibility for the human race as a whole, not for just a tiny bit of it.

If the only logical conclusion of oneness is world service, then world service is the surest path to oneness. And one of the finest ways to live this truth is by praying for the world as often and as powerfully as you can.

Ceramic from Herat, Afghanistan.

PRAYER CREDITS

Page 76: extracts from *The Rubais of Rumi* translated by Nevit O. Ergin and Will Johnson, Rochester, VT 05767, copyright © 2007 Inner Traditions/Bear and Co. (www.InnerTraditions.com).

Page 90: "Common Prayer" is reproduced from *Gems of Prayers* by Sri Swami Sivananda by kind permission of the publisher, the Divine Life Society.

Page 107: "A Vedic Prayer for Fearlessness" is reproduced from *The Vedic Experience* by Raimundo Panikkar by kind permission of Darton, Longman & Todd Ltd.

Page 108: "Affirmation of the Disciple" was originally published in *Telepathy and the Etheric Vehicle* by Alice Bailey and is reproduced by kind permission of the copyright holder the Lucis Trust (www.lucistrust.org).

Page 114: "Prayer for Very Small Children" by Rudolf Steiner was translated by Mark Bennett.

Page 118: "A Muslim Prayer about Love" is reproduced from *Selections from Rahman Baba* (translated by Jens Enevoldsen) by kind permission of Poul Kristensens Forlag, DK-Herning.

Page 134: "Oh Lord! I Surrender Myself unto Thee" is reproduced from *In the Hours of Communion* by Sri Swami Sivananda by kind permission of the publisher, the Divine Life Society.

Page 151: "Prayer for World Peace" is reproduced from *Gems of Prayers* by Sri Swami Sivananda by kind permission of the publisher, the Divine Life Society.

PHOTOGRAPH ACKNOWLEDGMENTS

p1 bronze statue of Buddha Ratnasanbhava, Tibet (10th century); Musée Guimet/Bonora/BAL; p2 "The Ancient of Days" by William Blake (1794); British Museum/akg/Erich Lessing; p3 detail from "Mary of the Annunciation" by Hans Strigel the Younger (1465); Staatsgalerie/akg; p5 detail from "Angel Holding an Olive Branch" by Hans Memling (15th century); Louvre/Giraudon/BAL; p6 detail from "Adoration of an Angel" by Fra Angelico (c.1430–40); Louvre/BAL; p8 detail from "Mary Admiring Jesus" by Fra Filippo Lippi (c.1459); akg/Orsi Battaglini; p9 National Museum, Paro, Bhutan/akg/Erich Lessing; p11 Metropolitan Museum of Art/BAL; p12 "Mandala of Amoghapasa", Nepalese School (19th century); Musée Guimet/BAL; p13 detail from "The Coronation of the Virgin Mary" by Dieric Bouts the Elder (1455); akg/Erich Lessing; p15 detail from "Deasa", Buddhist monks holding prayer beads, Korean School; Gahoe Museum, Jongno-gu, South Korea/BAL; p16 private collection/© Michael Graham-Stewart/BAL; p19 private collection/photo © Christie's Images/BAL; p20 San Vitale, Ravenna, Italy/BAL; p23 detail from "Madonna and Child" by Jacopo Palma (Il Vecchio) (15th century); private collection/photo © Christie's Images/BAL; pp25/26 Musée Guimet/BAL; p27 akg/Cameraphoto; p28 detail from "St Peter", Byzantine mosaic (c. CE 700); St Peter's, Vatican/BAL; p32 detail showing Egyptian pharoah Akehenaton, making offerings to the sun god (c.1350 BCE); National Museum, Cairo/akg/Erich Lessing; p35 Pinacoteca di Brera, Milan/akg/Erich Lessing; p36 Ajanta, Maharashtra, India/BAL; p37 detail from "The Coronation of the Virgin Mary" by Dieric Bouts the Elder (1455); akg/Erich Lessing; p38 National Gallery, London/akg/Erich Lessing; p41 private collection/BAL; p44 National Museum of Karachi/Giraudon/BAL; p45 detail of a Thangka, showing Amoghasiddhi, one of the five transcendental Buddhas, Tibet (late 14th

ivory plaque; akg/Erich Lessing; p143 Bibliotheque Nationale, Paris/BAL; p144 Johnny van Haeften Gallery, London/BAL; p147 National Museum, Damascus/akg/Jean-Louis Nou; p148 "A Choir of Angels" by Simon Marmion (1459); National Gallery, London/BAL; p149 photo © Southampton City Art Gallery, UK/BAL; p150 detail from "The Annunciation to Mary" by Simone Martini (1333); Galleria degli Uffizi, Florence/akg/Rabatti Domingie; p153 photo © Leeds Museums and Galleries (City Art Gallery)/BAL; p155 private collection/akg/Mörchel-Hartmann; p157 akg/Gerard Degeorge.

akg = akg-images
BAL = The Bridgeman Art Library

INDEX OF PRAYERS